Reviews for My

"Fascinating, exciting, anxiety   ⌐   ...·y, ·.·y funny...perfectly describes the multi-faceted way trauma affects people."

- **Consultant Psychiatrist**

"My heart was in my mouth as Joanne quite literally fell to earth; a brave and loving memoir that is testimony to her grit as a woman, wife, mother and leader. I couldn't put this book down and know that I will carry it with me."

- **PTSD survivor, extreme sports enthusiast, and mother**

"My Piece of Sky is a story of hope. Joanne's story is an inspiration to anyone who has been through extreme trauma or a near-death experience. For survivors and family members looking for help and support after a traumatic event, the author really shows that emotional and physical scars can be healed through love, determination, hard work, perseverance, and a positive outlook. This book is written in such an intimate way; openly, clearly and honestly. Joanne showcases how the wisdom gained during a near-death experience can be life-enhancing and have hugely positive

effects in one's life in the long-term. A must-read for anyone looking for hope in times of need and looking to overcome a difficult or emotional challenge in life. A must read."

- **Miriam Stevenson**

My Piece of Sky

Choosing Life

Recovering Body, Mind and Spirit

Joanne McConville

First Published in 2022 by Heather Shields Publishing

ISBN: 978-1-8383820-6-3

HeatherShieldsPublishing.com

About the Book

Ground rush is scary when green swirling grass comes up to grab you as you fall from 6,500 feet at over 100mph. You are plummeting towards your fate, not knowing what that will be. Will it be certain death, or will you survive to tell the tale? Unbelievably Joanne survived.

Her skydiving accident was one of those "before and after" moments in life, where in an instant all she knew had passed and she was forced down a new path to a world of survival, recovery, and insight.

Writing this book has enabled her to bring out the reality of the experience, the details of which have been hidden for years, from what led her to skydive, the accident and near-death experience, the ups and downs of recovery and the learnings she gained.

This book captures the full story 25 years on; it is especially for those who have experienced a traumatic event and those who treat them. Joanne shares the impact her accident had physically, mentally, and emotionally alongside the reality of everyday difficulties and triggers without any knowledge of what to expect, no access to information in a pre-internet age and no specialist support and treatment from the medical and therapeutic world. Through her own journey, determination and her experience as a healthcare professional Joanne has found a way through that she now hopes readers can benefit from, and healthcare professionals can build upon.

Joanne's message is one of hope and encouragement for others to dig deep and find all the resilience and strength they have within to recover from adversity and live the best life possible.

***Please note: If this story affects you in any way, please reach out to someone you can talk to, explore self-help options, use helplines, go to practitioners or organisations that offer specialist help and speak to your doctor or mental health services.*

You do not have to suffer trauma, and its side-effects, on your own, you are not alone.

About the Author

Joanne McConville is a healthcare professional from a nursing background, with over 30 years of experience in the UK's National Health Service, Private Sector and Civil Service. Her focus on coaching and developing excellent leadership practice led her to found Clarity Change, a consultancy supporting businesses to achieve this.

However, it was a passion for skydiving born out of a desire to help her son that led to a skydiving accident over 25 years ago that many thought she wouldn't, couldn't or even shouldn't survive.

Married to her skydiving instructor, Joe, for the past 25 years they have five children, grandchildren, and a home together close to the beautiful Lough Neagh in County Antrim, Northern Ireland.

By telling her inspirational personal story, combined with work and life experiences, Joanne provides inspirational talks, seminars, and development programmes on topics such as resilience, adaptability, trauma, learning from near-death experiences, leadership, how to thrive from difficult times and become the best person you can be, in all areas of your life.

Introduction

This book could have been a love story, an insight into what it is like to be faced with death and the trauma of its aftermath or the amazing experience of having a near-death experience and in the end, it became all three. Delving into the pages of the diary I kept in the first two years after my accident, talking to family and friends and reading through the vast amount of information there is on trauma and near-death experiences, my memories, good and bad, came flooding back to allow me to write an honest, open account of that time in my life 25 years ago.

By sharing my story in all its glorious, messy, terrifying, romantic, and uplifting highlights, I hope you will stop and think about what you would do if you had walked in my shoes at that time and what would be important to you. When everything I had in the world was stripped away, I gained an in-depth insight into myself for the first time and the values I live by were all I had left. I ask you to consider what would be most important to you and the values you have and live by.

In coming along with me on my journey I will be showing you much of the reality of when a great day skydiving turned into a nightmare accident on my 65th jump, falling from 6,500 feet and hitting the ground at over 100mph, staring death in the face and what it took to pick myself up and move on. I ask you to take away what is relevant to your life and the traumas or challenging times you or those close to you face or have faced, as I explain what I have learned and how the experience impacted on my life, then and now.

I was a nurse and at the time of my accident the Northern Ireland "Troubles" were ongoing. I had been used to seeing and treating traumatised patients, whether from "Trouble" related incidents or serious accidents and road traffic collisions, which I handled with the stoicism I needed to care for those who needed me. Through the book I will outline how my thought processes changed when I returned to nursing two years after my accident, including my nursing practice, thoughts around the dying process and the increased empathy and connection I had with my patients.

Over time my story has become a good tale to tell new acquaintances and work colleagues, concentrated on the positives and skirting around the details of my psychological and emotional suffering, so very few people have ever asked the questions that can lead to clarity, learning and ultimately change gained through an experience such as this.

Questions that can lead to Clarity:

 ❖ How did you get over it?

* How did you change?

* What did you learn?

* What would have helped you?

* What would you have done differently?

In hindsight if I had shared the wisdom I gained it may have made a difference to those working in healthcare and to individuals going through difficult times, and so it has become a goal of mine to increase knowledge amongst people who may provide care, or need care after such an event so they can communicate effectively, share information, give support and, in the case of the individual, find a way to live through recovery.

Lastly, I hope this book will inspire everyone who reads it, give hope to those going through their own trauma and let those who have had a near-death experience know they are not alone. Because this happened to me, I know it is possible to pick up the pieces, travel down a new path and live a life, to the best of your ability, full of love, laughter, endless possibilities, and build the resilience to overcome whatever you may face in the future.

Joanne McConville

Antrim, Northern Ireland

February 2022

This book is dedicated to:

Joe, my best friend, and soulmate,

My children, who kept me alive, and

My family and friends, who were always

there for me.

"All the world's a stage, and all the men and women merely players..."

- **Shakespeare**

The Cast

Meet the cast of this book...

The Leading roles:

Joe and I

Our Friends:	**Our Children:**	**My Family:**
Stevie	Aaron	Andrew (Father)
Paula	Matthew	June (Mother)
Willie	Alex	Karen (Sister)
Adam	Natalie	Robert (Brother)
And all the	Ella	
Blueskies Gang		

Contents

Act One

Opening the Circle

"… I came across a fallen tree

I felt the branches of it looking at me

Is this the place we used to love?

Is this the place that I've been dreaming of? …"

- **Somewhere only we know - Keane**

Chapter One

Why jump out of a

perfectly good plane?

People aren't made to freefall, it doesn't make rational sense to do it, we didn't evolve to fly, or jump off high levels just for excitement. That's why most sensible people keep their feet firmly planted on the ground. *So why on earth would I want to?* Skydiving wasn't a life-long dream for me, I didn't even like sports up to then, especially one deemed inappropriate for a woman, and definitely not for a mother. I was trying to think of ways to raise money for charity and needed to do something big to make a difference, for my son and other families struggling to have a "normal" life with a physically disabled child.

Like thousands of people every year, I chose jumping out of a plane, with no intention of ever doing more than one. I remember travelling the seventy miles from home to the parachute club; my friend, who was doing her first jump with me, and I were feeling the entangled excitement and fear building up as never before. We were both repeating, *"What are we doing? Should we turn round, it's not too late?"*, but no, we drove on. I had come to raise charity money so I couldn't pull out and face those who had sponsored me. I didn't know how much I would come to love it, right from the first jump, so that I did it again that first day, and sixty-four more times after that.

The reason was clear to me. My two oldest children and I had almost become residents in the children's ward in Musgrave Park Hospital in Belfast for the past several years. They were both born with hip dysplasia where their hip sockets didn't form properly. The MITRE Trust was set up in the hospital and I was hoping that some of the money raised would be spent on new equipment to make life easier for the children and parents when they left the hospital. There were no wheelchairs that children could lay back on and it wasn't until they were out of plasters and could sit up again that we could all do the things that other families take for granted.

Aaron was born first in 1986 and at his 7-day check he was found to have "clicky hips". I was still in hospital, at that time there was no such thing as straight home as soon as you left the delivery suite, you stayed for 10 days. There was a one-hour opportunity for you to have your child beside your bed in the morning, and for visiting time in the afternoon. The rest of the time the babies were in the nursery in a row, you were discouraged from lifting them before feeding time, "just in case they became spoilt", no "demand feeding" and you certainly didn't put them on their back to sleep. On many occasions I found Aaron in a bundle of blankets at the bottom of the cot and the cot had been tipped and left beside running water, which was meant to soothe him so he would fall asleep on his own. I couldn't stand it. I was a permanent fixture in the nursery and couldn't wait to get him home, even if I didn't quite know what to do with him. It was so bad that when he was handed to me at first, I didn't know how to put him down, so I rolled him down my arms into the cot. I was eighteen, newly married, away from my family and completely naive when it came to babies.

We were transferred to Musgrave Park hospital that week and Aaron was put into traction, his legs suspended from a bar across the top of the cot to stretch the muscles in the inside of his groin so that they could be operated on to let his hip move back into its socket. After a couple of months, he came home in a harness that kept his legs apart so they could develop normally. Thankfully, they did as his condition was caught quickly, and he had no long-lasting difficulties.

Matthew was born 20 months later, and I so wanted him to have a normal babyhood. The routine hip test was apparently fine, but they referred me to the consultant who had treated Aaron, just as a precaution. He told me not to worry, that it would be very unusual for both children to have the same problem, so no X-rays or scans were taken. I just knew instinctively that there was something wrong as his hips and upper legs were out of shape and his left leg was shorter than the right. I hounded my doctor for 6 months until he agreed to order an X-ray. I don't know if anyone expected what it revealed, Matthew had a much more serious hip problem than Aaron. Both hips were dislocated, and his hip sockets could hardly be seen. Ligaments had grown into the space where the hip sockets should have been, it was obvious from the start that this was serious and extensive surgery and treatment would be needed. I was devasted and furious that he hadn't been diagnosed earlier, but I didn't have the assertiveness, or knowledge to question the decisions that the consultants had made. I sat in a haze as the consultant explained that he was unlikely to walk without difficulty, if he could at all, and would not be able to run. On one hand I was so relieved he didn't have a serious illness or disease that could threaten his life, but on the other hand I knew his life would be forever restricted.

For the next couple of years, he needed multiple surgeries and plaster casts from his chest down or just on his legs with a bar keeping his legs wide apart. He became famous in Musgrave Park and the star of the ward as there were only a few children who needed so much surgery or spent so long in hospital. We were so lucky Matthew bounced back from surgery and was renowned for his ringlets, big brown eyes and how cheerful he always was. His first four years continued to consist of surgeries and many stays in hospital.

Getting Matthew home in the large plasters was so awkward. In hospital he lay on an old-fashioned pram, tied on with straps, but when he had the full body plaster, he couldn't sit up and there was no car-seat or buggy that would take him. As he got bigger and heavier this was a major problem as it severely restricted how we went out, if at all, and how he was transported. He still remembers the back seat being put down so that his bottom half was in the boot and his head poking out in the front. Without this Aaron wouldn't have been able to get in and we wouldn't have been able to go out to do any normal activities. On the other hand, I remember finding him after he slid into the bath to play with his brother, in full plaster cast, taking him out and draining out the water by tipping him upside down and drying him with a hairdryer before taking him back to the hospital to be replastered. Matthew had his last major surgery when he was 8 years and, as an adult, he has had hip replacements and continues to be the inspiration he has always been.

So why jump for the first time? The money of course.

Why jump out of a perfectly good plane … again?

Skydiving is such an unnatural thing to do and totally goes against the primal fear instinct that is to help us survive; the fight, flight or freeze response. For those who love the sport it's impossible not to associate it with excitement and an adrenaline rush, the brain gives your body a mass injection of energy, strength, and speed in case you need these to survive. It's easy to see this response when people come to skydive, especially for the first time, some will freeze, unable to get out the door of the plane, some will refuse to get into the plane in the first place, some definitely run back to their cars and speed off, and others will outwardly show no signs of fear, learn to override the natural response and go for the thrill of the jump instead.

I was in the last category until I found out that this normal response, in an extreme situation that you can't get out of, when you are sure that death is unavoidable and when there's nothing left to help you survive, the brain switches to overdrive and takes you to places that will change your life forever. I have come to understand that what is experienced at this time cannot be explained away by an individual's response to stress or physical changes in the brain, but a myriad of possibilities outside human comprehension in a universe much, much bigger than one person on their own.

When those who had never jumped ask me *"what does it feel like"* and *"why did you do it?"*, it can be difficult to put into words, its indescribable, and each person will have a different experience, so *"you just have to do it to know"* was my usual reply. Among the other skydivers there were many familiar replies, *"because I can"*, *"because it has no door"*, *"because we love it"* and the usual man macho banter always *"it's better than sex!"*. This always made me laugh, thinking, they haven't been with the right partners then. There was also the fallacy, *"it's safer than crossing the road"*, that I now know is definitely not true, but I bought into at the beginning, just as many students do. You trust the instructors, practice the safety drills until they are ingrained in your mind and follow the rules, so it's bound to be safe…isn't it?

Safety was all I thought about in the early days, especially when I saw our plane, a little black Cesna 182 we called "GAVID", for the first time. I wondered would it still able to take off at all. Three people in full parachuting kit, plus the pilot, squeezed in like sardines in a tin and I soon realised the plane safety hardly counted if you have a mad pilot, adrenaline junkies and a multitude of things that could go wrong at any stage, not just on take-off.

Skydiving is like having two experiences in one jump. From the minute you leave the plane, everything else fades into insignificance and you're totally focused, engrossed in what you are doing and feeling.

Freefall is fast, it's scary, it's exhilarating, it's exciting, its nerve-wracking, and a brilliant experience.

Imagine being in an open topped car, standing with your hands in the air as fast as fast as it can go – that's nearly it. The noise is deafening, as noisy as standing beside speakers at a concert, so loud it's not possible to hear anything, or anyone, else, but this fades in time, or you don't notice it as much. Anything you haven't wrapped up is freezing, but you don't notice until you land, and fingers feel like they are broken when they begin to warm up. And then there is the smell of perfectly crisp fresh air, wonderful, untainted by any other smell, like breathing in on the top of a mountain on a cold day.

Suddenly, the fall stops as the parachute inflates. You can breathe again, relief that the parachute has opened, there were no serious malfunctions, you have time to get your bearings and plan your landing. Under the canopy feels serene, quiet, and peaceful, except for the sound of the canopy cells rippling as the air flows through, and you relax as you float down to a large white "X" on the ground. Your landing spot. You learn how to steer, and it becomes automatic after a while.

Bishopscourt was one of the most beautiful places to jump, a kaleidoscope of all good things; to one side the Irish Sea backed by the majesty of the Mourne Mountains, green fields, undulating hills, trees and a quiet openness that felt calm amongst the excitement of the club. In freefall and under the canopy we were part of the scenery, suspended above the world, looking down and just in awe of what we were seeing below. It is a proper birds-eye view and nothing like peering out from the window of a plane, nothing in between to spoil our view. It is only when your parachute opens, and you have time to take it in and see the beauty as you float, gently descending back to reality, that you can fully appreciate what you are seeing.

And then the landing, the final time things could go seriously wrong, misjudged height or turning into the wind too late to slow down, can lead to crashing into the ground, broken bones and certainly not the tiptoe landing you had planned.

The whole experience is a sensory overload, you are alive in every sense of the word.

The real rush always comes after you land and realise you are alive and unhurt – a surge of energy and elation hits. Jumpers become aware they have survived immediately, there is obvious relief and a wave of dopamine – the feel-good neurotransmitter, the human heroin, that produces a euphoric, natural high, and runs right through your body and is totally addictive. I knew that every jump would be slightly, or completely, different and that buzz was the gift that kept on giving.

I wanted excitement and escape for the first time in my life, and I had found it. At this time, I believed that fear was there to be controlled and this made me feel powerful and filled me with adventure; even when I wasn't jumping, I could feel the excitement. Life events until then had drained those feelings, in fact I didn't know that a life like this could exist. For me it was life-changing, positive, boosted my self-esteem and made me courageous, helping me to move out of my comfort zone, test my limits and learn about myself and what I wanted from life in the process. Regardless of the preconceived norms at the time, I heard often from others, that women had no place in dangerous sports, and certainly not if they had children, I felt, and still do, that it made me a better mother. My mindset positively changed, and I was both physically and psychologically stronger, not only in this part of my life, but in every aspect. I felt like a sky-goddess; strong, invincible, confident.

There are jumps that stand out for everyone, but working my way through the student categories, I had my favourites. Of course, the first jump will always be memorable, a one-off for most people, but I was hooked immediately. I did a static line jump, where you jump out on your own, with only as long as it takes for your parachute to open without something above your head, usually around three seconds. You have no idea what longer in freefall would be like, but doing the training with the build-up of excitement, climbing up to height in the plane, getting out onto a small step, letting go of the strut under the wing of the plane and falling backwards, coupled with the fear of everything that could go wrong rushing through your brain, is enough to begin with.

Having progressed from relying on a static line to first freefall is another momentous jump for anyone. What happens is all on you - a handle to pull to open your 'chute, with timing, body position and emergency routines to remember. Greater risk, but a far better buzz. Every good jump led to a new experience, and I just couldn't wait for the next one.

The next milestone is when you reach 10 seconds in freefall, falling 1,500 feet and facing earth for the first time. It is like speeding over the brow of a hill - that feeling of your stomach jumping into your mouth. This is the first experience of the effects of terminal velocity, when gravity is pulling you down towards earth, building up speed as you fall until it equals air resistance pushing upwards in total equilibrium and you will be reaching speeds of up to 120mph.

At that height the ground looks far away, and you believe you have more time than you do. It is a mismatch of knowing that you are falling, but your mind and body not recognising this; your logic and the illogical are trying to fit together but they just can't click into place. It is only as a jumper gets more experienced and the time-delays get longer that the phenomenon of terminal velocity can be used, with the airflow, to full advantage, with a change in body position to turn, speed up and manoeuvre with others becomes natural. By this time the jumper will be reliant on their altimeter and the horizon moving upwards to alert them to their opening height and keep them aware they are falling.

My all-time favourite jump was the "unstable exit" the aim being to roll up in a ball on the step with an instructor pushing you off to see if you could stop yourself spinning and tumbling, completely out of control, and stabilise back into a normal body position before opening the parachute. This is the only jump I wanted to do repeatedly. In reality, most of my freefalls were like this, but not on purpose.

Everything about freefall is risk management, but with risk comes reward and the reward is the adrenalin rush, as I progressed to longer times in freefall, I felt it more and more and it became a passion, a feeling of being totally alive. I know that this perfect picture is not always true.

Danger is always there, but by the time of the accident I wasn't a novice, having completed sixty-four jumps, and had lulled myself into the false belief that nothing big would ever happen to me... but it did. *So why jump again?* For the buzz of it.

Why jump out of a perfectly good plane... again and again?

It was all about the internal transformation, the power and accomplishment I felt, the drive and determination to nail each jump, the enjoyment of the lifestyle involved and the friends I made.

And then, of course, there was Joe, who became my friend first, boyfriend, my skydiving instructor and after a few years, my husband.

It's hard to know how long I would have stayed in the skydiving scene if we hadn't met and stayed together. *Was it Joe or the skydiving I loved so much, or both?* The skydiving was only a passing phase, the catalyst for the partnership we still have now.

We met in November 1992 by chance. It was a coincidence that we lived in the same town and came across each other at all as he would usually have been at the skydiving club on a Saturday night, but he had missed his lift and was drowning his sorrows in a local pub. He would say now it was love, or probably lust in his case, at first sight but it certainly wasn't for me. He looked like a scruffy 1970s leftover, dark longish curly hair and a moustache that took over his top lip. I told him he needed a shave and he said, "so do you". How rude! and as I'm sure you'll understand, that was the end of that conversation. Little did we know then that we would experience so much in the first years of our relationship, we bonded in an accident that we went through together and would have to fight to stay together through the trauma we both felt afterwards.

I didn't see him again for another year when I went to do that fateful first jump. Joe was helping with the course and every break we had he was there, flirty, and cheeky until he wore me down, the spark was igniting and over the next few months we got to know each other better at the club and in the pub where we first met.

The rest of our love story is history. We were soulmates, intensely and passionately in love, wrapped up in each other, the skydiving world, our friends, our homelife and everything else just made sense. Living together seemed the obvious next step, Joe moved in around nine months before the accident, bringing together his daughter, Natalie, from his first marriage and Aaron, Matthew, and Alex from mine to become a new family. We were lucky this all went well, the kids got on with no labels of stepbrother or stepsister, just siblings, and Joe's and my relationship became stronger and stronger. We were still in the "honeymoon period", ready to forgive or overlook any differences we had and with rows and make-ups equally as intense. We had no idea at that time that staying together in the aftermath of the accident, and the extreme pressure that this would put on us, would benefit from the foundations we had already built, a shared passion for jumping, a deep love, the belief that we would stay together forever and the importance we placed on making a stable life for our children.

All the characters I met through skydiving also kept me there. Blueskies club attracted many people looking for something that would give the ultimate high, or those who felt they didn't fit in anywhere in other areas of their lives. People that otherwise probably would not have got to know each other; from all backgrounds, situations, relationships – good and bad, all came with an individual reason to pick this as a pastime.

During my years at the club, I built true friendships that have lasted a lifetime, the type you know will be at the end of a telephone whenever you need them, know more about you than your family, accept you the way you are and who you can trust implicitly. They understood why the pull of skydiving was so strong and, for me, were there holding my hand and keeping me safe on the day of my accident - and still support me now.

There was such a bond between us all, as is often the case with this type of sport. This was our group, our tribe. Skydiving is a very selfish sport, with every single aspect of our lives geared towards our next jump and we spent a lot of time together. We waited for a break in the weather or clouds together, looked after each other through thick and thin and budding relationships, long-term commitments and love all began at the Blueskies Club in Bishopscourt. There was feeling of acceptance of one another that excluded everyone else who was not involved. Looking back, with some embarrassment I now recognise that when we were out as a group we probably sounded like arrogant prats, talking about jumping like there was nothing better in the world and yet dying for someone to come over to ask what it was like so that we could show off. We had a cocky self-belief, some would call it arrogance, that we were somewhat better than everyone else because we were adrenaline junkies, doing something others wouldn't dare, especially in Northern

Ireland where skydiving is such a small sport. We thought we were excluding others because they wouldn't be interesting enough, but others were probably trying to avoid us at all costs.

However, time spent at the club excluded other parts of my life as I would be away from home for hours waiting for the clouds to clear, or to get enough height to make a jump worthwhile. Any extra penny I had was saved for a jump and it was like an addiction that I didn't want to give up and couldn't wait to do again. It was three years of my life that suited me at that time and wouldn't have at any other, or since.

So why jump again and again? For love and friendships.

Chapter Two

The Return

I'm not sure what made me go back. I had always thought someday, someday I will make the journey but just not today. In the first year after the accident a few awkward trips back to Bishopscourt had revealed to me that my place was now very much on the side-lines, I could be a spectator but never part of this scene again. In the times I went back, in those early days, I had never walked down to the end of the runway, to the actual spot where I landed. On one of those trips, I was looking out from the Parachute Centre in the direction of the place I landed at the end of the runway when, in a moment of dark humour, one of the jumpers spoke into my ear. *"Do you know you made a divot in the ground over there?"*

I looked round and laughed at the typically dark humour, but the enormity of it hit me – I immediately remembered lying in that divot, surrounded by small bushes and a stony mound that I had bounced on first, lifting into the air, before landing for the final time. Behind the laugh I was thinking *"if only he knew what an insignificant detail that is compared to what I'm going through now"*, but still, I was overwhelmed at the thought that I landed so hard and fast that I had made an actual shape in the ground. I knew then that I couldn't go to the actual site at the end of the runway, and may never go, it was just too soon, too raw, I didn't want to see it. Physically my body couldn't take me there, and mentally I didn't want to go.

As the years unfolded, I didn't put the return off for any particular reason, but I never made it happen. In the first few years it would have been too much to take in, and in the years that followed there seemed to be less and less need to go.

When the silver anniversary of the accident passed, I realised that I had lived with negative memories of trauma and positive ones of a profoundly life-changing near-death experience for a quarter of a century, nearly half my lifetime Throughout the distraction of recovery, building a career and the practicality and main focus of bringing up my children to give them all that I possibly could, meant I never had the luxury of taking time out for myself. I avoided delving in too deep, not knowing what would happen if I did, and keeping busy was a distraction from the memories that were too difficult to think of. After all, look what had happened the last time I had taken time for myself to pursue a hobby I loved.

My current life was in transition, and I knew I had no option but to change direction, I was disappointed that my career in the NHS had not ended in the way I thought it would. I was worn out and, although I was ambitious, and had worked my way up to become a senior manager in the NHS, I wasn't fulfilled and had stopped enjoying my work, and ultimately my home-life suffered, as did my mental health. So, I walked away, left the good salary and pension, not knowing what I would do, but also determined to finally find something that I would find more fulfilling, that it was my time.

This was a scary proposition, uncertainty and such radical change always is, and I felt like I had gone back to the immediate aftermath of the accident when I had to find courage to move on, lift my self-esteem and confidence and change my plans for the future. But this time I knew it was up to me, that I could do it and had all the resilience and experience I would need to turn this situation around and lead myself into the next chapter of my life.

As soon as I got off the mad work treadmill, the accident and all its repercussions seemed ever-present, intruding on my thoughts. This had happened many times over the years when I struggled with depression. I would begin to spiral into dark thoughts and focus on negative events in my life, the accident being the main one, remembering the pain and struggle it had been to recover and seldom the unbelievable fact that I had survived when I shouldn't have and was given years more to live, and all that I had achieved in my life. This was an opportunity to really explore what I would like to do next. I did things I had never considered before, such as becoming a hypnotherapist and a coach and starting a business of my own based on my career in healthcare and leadership. I realised that no matter what I had done with my life to date, the learning and understanding I had gained through that one experience could have the most positive impact on others in similar situations and be cathartic for me in the process.

I knew I had always wanted to capture my accident, and recovery, in a book and I had the diary I had kept in the year afterward to refer to. The diary was always there, in a box full of everything I kept as special over the years and brought with us through each of our numerous house moves; cards from when the children were born, their first curls and teeth, handprints from nursery, school reports and my one and only love letter from Joe. The box is seldom opened, but I know it's there, like a comfort blanket. When I pulled out the diary and began to read, I felt so connected to that time in my life, like putting my hand out to touch my 27-year-old self and a life that I hardly recognised yet was familiar. Memories came flooding back of that time in my life, hectic and always full, raising young children, trying to start a career, full and part-time work, studying for a degree, building a new relationship after the failure of my first marriage, always looking for the next thing and always pushing forwards. It makes me exhausted just thinking about it now.

In this diary was the physically and mentally broken me; angry, frustrated, confused, and scared, with an uncertain future, a person that I don't recognise now. It captured the year after the accident, the physical and mental trauma and none of the positives that were also there. I had only written down the parts I couldn't share with others, the hidden demons, my true feelings of the harsh reality of what trauma can do to your mind, relationships, and your future.

I'd never written a book before, it's a marathon, not a walk in the park, but what a learning curve it has been. I had heard that "everyone has a least one good story in them", this would be mine and it felt like I was beginning a circle, one that would be complete when the story was told.

As I looked at the blank page in front of me, not knowing where to start or what I wanted to say, the best way I could think to bring back memories and get the creative juices flowing, was to revisit the site of the accident. As mad as this sounds, to go back to a place that holds many traumatic memories, I was curious and wanted to see what I would think and how I would react if I went to the spot where it all happened. Of course, I was anxious and fearful. *"What if I opened Pandora's box and the horrific memories spilled out? What if I was still traumatised after all this time without being aware of it and regretted ever going?"* Despite this I was also thinking, *"Can I finally find out if this really happened to me, acknowledge that it was real and maybe put it to bed for the last time?"*

I was lying in bed as the sun came up, thinking about the book, when the light streamed through the curtains on a bright and sunny autumnal day, a blue-sky day, just like the day of the accident. I knew then that this would be the day I finally went back. My husband Joe and daughter Ella were in the kitchen when I came bouncing down the stairs in one of my overly motivated, high-energy, "I'm not taking any crap from anyone today" moods.

"Right, we are going down to visit Bishopscourt, I must see it, and I want to go the actual spot. You're both coming with me". Within 30 minutes we were in the car.

I was thinking of this time in my life the whole journey to Bishopscourt and how the story, and any details of how traumatic it was, had been edited throughout the years. In the days after the accident, when I saw the reaction of others and felt the extreme trauma myself, I decided the story I told in the future would exclude the gory details, the horrific truth, what I actually felt like when faced with death and instead let those who asked create a vision in their own head, picture the scene and make up their own mind of how they would feel or think at a time like that. This proved to be enough, protecting me, and those around me, knowing I could tell an adapted version of the truth, with physical injuries and an incredible near-death experience becoming the stars of the show.

Even to this day no matter how many times I recount the complete story, outwardly calm and detached, the invisible familiar feelings are always there of remembered trauma, fear, the beat of my heart speeding up and sickness to the pit of my stomach coming dangerously close to the surface, threatening to shock those listening, stumbling to phrase my feelings, terrified I would unleash a monster too big for me to control. I became an expert in swallowing it all down without choking, chaining it back into the dark recesses of my mind. Back where it belonged. Over the years I had gotten so good at it, it became the norm, just like learning to conquer fear every time I jumped, I would be able to control the real emotion.

The tale had become robotic and well-rehearsed, until I began to imagine it was only a dream that had happened to someone else, but that has never completely worked. The sneering, laughing voice inside my head reminds me I can't escape from the trauma that easily, it's not going to disappear no matter how I try. It has always been a constant tug of war, sometimes the voice wins, but, thankfully, more often I have over the years. The events are always there, like a heavy pressure around my chest and heart.

But then there is the near-death experience (NDE), the most profound experience of my life and a major part of the story, mixed up in the trauma. Unbelievable but true. Both are integral to the experience, the negative trauma and positive near-death experience that caused the psychological responses I had immediately afterwards, and that are still part of my daily life today. Out of all the memories, the vision and smell and beauty of the near-death experience is the most vivid. It sticks in my mind as if it was just yesterday and hasn't dulled with time, like the memories of the pain of physical injuries or some events and details from around that time, have.

There was a palpable feeling of trepidation in the car, and I could sense that both Joe and Ella were becoming more anxious as we continued to drive, probably uncertain of how we would react. I think Ella was nervous for both of us, but on some level, excited to see what all the fuss was about. She had heard the stories for as long as she could remember but had little insight into the sport and lifestyle that had been a major part of our lives before she was born. The boys and Natalie had been fully immersed in the experience of the drop zone and we didn't know what she would feel about her first time there.

For Joe, revisiting was going to be as challenging as it was for me.

We were the only two people who knew exactly what had happened that day and even though the physical injuries happened to me, it must have been horrific for him too. Over the years the whole story focused on my experience, this took precedent and was all anyone else wanted to know about, and his story was almost forgotten along the way. We handled the aftermath of the accident so differently and he had never totally opened up about how he had actually felt in the air that day, watching me plummet to the ground, unable to help me, I didn't know what this would bring up for him and hoped I wasn't forcing him into a situation that he wasn't ready for.

The road down was so familiar, like I had never been away. Joe and I looked at each other and I knew we were thinking the same thing and that we could both feel the excitement and controlled fear mounting, just as it used to do when we knew we were going to the club to jump. When we got to Downpatrick, 5 miles from the drop zone, I could see the hairs were standing up on Joe's arms and I began to feel nervousness and anxiety building up inside me too.

Travelling through Downpatrick, Ella heard the old stories as we reminisced about parties in the pubs and the "greedy pig" breakfasts, on pig shaped plates, we had after a good night out to line our stomachs ready for jumping. There were quite a few hangovers fixed this way, but others were only resolved by free-falling as there is nothing better than jumping out of a plane to clear your head. Some of those hangovers lasted until freefall was over unfortunately. Thankfully, we didn't have to be tested for alcohol levels to fly a parachute or we would have been well over the legal limit.

The road twisted and turned from Downpatrick to Ballyhornan and with each twist and turn my memory and emotions, that had been supressed for so long, began to bubble up to the surface from my subconscious mind. Every pothole and twist in the road brought me back to the ambulance ride from the drop zone to Downpatrick Hospital and how very jolt and turn caused more pain. As I lay in the back of the ambulance, sucking on gas and air, noticing the unnerving silence, the grave faces of the paramedics and the fear etched on Joe's face, it had seemed to be the longest journey of my life. As I was topped up with morphine thinking, *"I'm having a party here, high as a kite, but no one else is joining in"*.

Today the journey down this road felt the same, it was taking forever and giving me plenty of time to consider reversing my need to return to Bishopscourt and go back home. *"Why was I doing this? What was I trying to prove and why put myself through it?"* The doubts and fears were creeping in as I began to feel more and more nervous of the unknown.

Yet I didn't return home, it was now or never, we kept going until we were finally there.

The airfield was disserted when we arrived, but the gates were open, we drove in and down the racetrack that used to be our runway. As soon as we got out of the car, 25 years later, everything felt familiar. It was a day like it had been on the day of the accident, a clear blue sky, but this was autumnal rather than the first smell of spring. It was such a large space that had changed little; the building we had used as a clubhouse was still there, the control tower in the distance and even the windsock remained. It was quiet and peaceful, a flat expanse, an old airfield built in WW2, with little interference from the world outside over the years since. You could hear a gentle buzz of a car going past or work going on in the distance, but mostly it was very, very still. I could see why I would be attracted to that at that time in my life, as when you weren't jumping you could often just go somewhere on your own to think, sort out problems in your mind or if you wanted to, scream or cry, without anyone knowing.

What did shock me, as I looked around, was how close many hazards were that we had to avoid when we were landing. I had always thought the houses in Ballyhornan village were further away, that we had plenty of room to land and the runways were far from where I had had my accident, but jumpers rarely landed too far off the drop zone and accidents were few and far between.

When I had first started jumping the club was based in Eglinton airport close to Londonderry, and soon after the club moved to Bishopscourt. Just like learning to drive, we had to be taught to fly the parachute to make sure we were able to land properly, and in the right place. At first students were guided to land, with instruction from an instructor on the ground using a one-way radio. This was a saving grace, but also meant you got dependent on those talking you down and didn't get used to manoeuvring the canopy yourself as quickly as you could have. I had started jumping with large green T10 parachutes, the circular ones you see in old war movies, not the stylish, high performing ones James Bond has under his suit. The T10s only had basic control, left and right, but no brakes to let you land on your feet. Despite hours practising the perfect way to land, I always landed like a sack of potatoes, rather than a nice, safe and lady-like elegant roll.

There are many memories that are hilarious in hindsight but were not necessarily so at the time. Once, my friends and I landed in a field of hay with large, tightly rolled cylinder-shaped hay bales scattered all over. As usual I landed in a heap; feet, ankles, bum, back then head and lay on the ground a bit too long before collapsing my canopy. The canopy filled with air again and before I could stand, I was dragged along the field, laughing so much I couldn't get up. The other two jumpers landed in the same field and were running to catch me, but I only stopped because the lines of the chute went round one of the hay bales and I was impaled against it like a cartoon character. We had to walk for ages and climb over a barbed wire fence to get back to the drop zone. No one back at the club was worried about us, or was going to come to get us, they just wanted to know the canopies hadn't been damaged.

We also travelled to other skydiving clubs. I have vivid memories of a road trip to Strathallan Parachute Club in Scotland. Unfortunately, they did not use those one-way radios to the same extent as Blueskies, students were left to get themselves back to the drop zone. Big mistake! We had been warned not to land outside of the drop zone; as they were having problems with local farmers due to students landing in their fields, wrecking their crops, or scaring the animals. I got out on a cloudy day and fell through the clouds, but when I came out of them, I was miles away from the drop zone and ended up landing in someone's back garden as they had a BBQ … I don't know what all the fuss was about as I was giving them free entertainment and at least I didn't fall on their roof or car. You can imagine the reaction I got when I arrived back to the drop zone, nearly being barred from jumping there again.

Luckily most of the "demos" by the experienced jumpers went to plan. This is when the sky gods of the club got to show off to the public and bask in the glory of skydiving. They were hired to jump into events and there was never a problem saying yes. Generally, everyone landed in the right place, just a few mishaps, like landing at a wedding or past the landing spot in Falls Park in Belfast into the crowd. By far, the funniest place Joe landed with two others, was onto a tiny island just off Ballyhornan Beach. Who jumps intentionally onto an island without organising a boat to collect them?! I think there was a lot of laughing and quite a few pints before anyone decided to rescue them.

Facilities at the drop zone were basic. There were toilets but only cold water to wash in. There were no streetlights so when it got dark, it was really dark. We all slept in a concrete bunker powered by a generator, that had to be turned off at some point in the night so that we were relying on torches, or just not moving, until it went on again in the morning. You never knew who you would wake up beside, or how many heads would be sticking out of a sleeping bag the next day. Luckily, I had Joe and he had me, and this is where our new relationship grew and blossomed, but there certainly wasn't much privacy for romance.

The boys' memories of that time are of the skydiving club as the ultimate playground. Aaron thought it was brilliant to be able to go into school on Monday mornings and tell everyone he had been packing parachutes all weekend and watching people jump out of planes. There weren't many of his friends who did anything so exciting and different, they were going to McDonald's and playing football. Even so, the boys weren't at the drop zone every weekend as they also spent time with their father and with their grandparents. Natalie, who was a teenager at the time of my accident, was certainly not interested in life in a drop zone anymore, and she came down to the club less and less.

The boys were all under 10 years old, and they couldn't be watched constantly when we were there, they were always getting up to mischief. There were fields to play in and with lots happening they always had something to watch, experience or be part of. It is only lately that they have told me all their stories and the dangerous things they got up to would make your hair stand on end. Aaron told me they ran back and forward over the runway, playing chicken with the plane as it landed, shocking as I thought I had kept a very close eye on what they were up to.

In the training room we had a "mock-up" plane, a wooden version of the inside and outside of the plane, with an open door and the inside the shape of the fuselage so students could practice getting out and know what to expect. At night there was always a rush to make sure you got to sleep in it, as it was much better than the practice mats on a concrete floor. The boys loved this mock-up. They became pilots, instructors and students and were continually jumping in and out to see who could jump the furthest. The "creepers" were also an endless source of fun. These are low X-shaped wooden structures with wheels attached for experienced jumpers to practice the moves they were going to do in freefall, and the formations they were going to get into. The boys would spin and pull each other round the clubhouse until we got fed up with them and put the creepers away.

Having the boys there also came in very useful. The instructors used the boys to demonstrate how to do a perfect landing, or Parachute Landing Fall (PLF)'s to students. They also had tiny hands to fix parachutes into the bags but the part they loved the most was the most disgusting job that no one else wanted to do.

We had a set of wooden stocks at the club. Everyone who did something momentous, like their first freefall, or their 100th jump, would be stripped and stuck in the stocks. It was like a "passing out parade" or equivalent to getting a badge of honour. The unlucky person was then covered with anything we could lay our hands on, and when the boys were there, they were sent off with a bucket and shovel to gather sheep dung, old food, and anything else that was lying around that you wouldn't want to get thrown over you. There were also army tents to camp out in and a caravan with an endless supply of food, sweets, and drinks – kiddie heaven.

In joining us on this return trip Ella, saw for the first time the place that held many memories for her father, siblings and I, a world that she was never part of. I had her five years after my accident and she grew up later than our other children, who were so involved in it all. They had seen the younger versions of me, full of energy, with the hectic life, the fun times, and the upsetting ones too. They saw, and lived through, the aftermath of the accident; watching me on crutches, sore and incapable of helping them out as much as I used to, having to grow up faster than they normally would. Through it all they were no trouble, soon able to make a good cup of tea and get their own breakfast; they appeared to take on the greater independence with acceptance – they got on with it as kids do and they say they can't remember the years after the accident being difficult or noticing anything changing that much. Alex was too small to remember, but Aaron and Matthew weren't and although they don't go into it in depth with me, it must have been a major event in their childhood and impact on their lives.

The Spot

Reminiscing was all very well, but we were there for a reason, and the time had come to go to the site. I felt like I was dragging my feet down towards the end of the familiar runway, a whole mixture of feelings, from curiosity, to fear and trepidation. All three of us walked silently, focused on where we were heading, lost in our thoughts. For me, the surroundings faded as I concentrated on the circle of tall trees in the distance. *Should I carry on, or run back to the car?* If I ran away, I knew I would never come back again or find out how I would react. *Would I still feel traumatised and was I testing myself to see if I was over it?* I felt if this caused too much trauma, I would certainly not be able to write the book I wanted to and I knew I would be disappointed in the future. A lot hinged on how this went.

Finally, we were there. I had forgotten that in 25 years the small saplings that had been there at that time would now be tall trees and found the ground beneath them covered in thorny blackberry bushes, tall grass, and nettles.

I paused before I went in, taking it all in, turning to look at the surroundings. These trees were the only ones for as far as the eye could see, somehow out of place, at the point where two runways crossed over each other only a hundred metres away from my landing spot, unbelievably close. I had landed in probably the safest place, a place of green surrounded by concrete.

As much as Joe wanted to support me, he didn't want to come through the trees with me and that was when I realised, maybe for the first time, how the visions of what he saw that day and the awful memories he had when he was last there must still be haunting him and I vowed that his voice would also be heard in this story.

Ella and I stumbled through the undergrowth, passing between the trees through to a clearing. I recognised the spot where I had landed instantly, a small clearing with two little mounds of stones and grass. These weren't covered in the same amount of undergrowth, so were easy to see. What struck me was the quietness and peace of the clearing, but maybe I had zoned out from any outside noise, I was focused on the moment. The place reminded me of an old overgrown churchyard protected by a falling-down stone wall and ruined church. It felt almost spiritual, magical, with the trees bending inwards, protecting the clearing, maybe waiting for me to come back. Having grown up in the country I recognised the smells of wet grass, tree bark and could see the tracks of wildlife, maybe a fox or rabbit that spoiled the feeling that nothing, or no one, had been there for years.

Standing there was surreal, like a dream that I knew I had had, but at the same time believing that something like that couldn't have happened to me, even though I could feel the physical and psychological repercussions every day. I was totally overwhelmed by the level of emotion I felt. I could remember everything, as if my whole self was re-experiencing the accident. This wasn't just remembering an event; I could, once again, feel the physical pain, my body ached, and the smell of fresh blood overwhelmed me. I unconsciously felt for my teeth with my tongue – this time they were there, not broken and bleeding. I could feel the emotions of the pure horror of the fall, and I could see flashes of the ground swirling before me as it had in the seconds before I hit the ground. I remembered the sounds; the people rushing to my side, the smell of the grass and soil and lying on my back, in shock that I had survived.

Time seemed to stand still as I fought to regain control, but in that moment, I felt jolted into reality; the accident had happened to me and not someone else, it wasn't a bad dream. I had lived when so many other people would not have. I could now understand and accept that it was the brutal landing and the trauma to my body and mind that was causing the physical pain that I live with now, however, the shocker was how quickly I dissolved into my memories, reopening old wounds, and it was scary. I realised that I still concentrated on the physical injuries, with a new recognition that the psychological side of the trauma had not been considered or dealt with over the years. I hadn't expected to react in such a way, or for my feelings be so real and it was then I realised that the traumatic side of the story would be very difficult to tell. I felt a roller-coaster of emotions, but no matter how hard it was going to be I knew that I wanted to delve into my memories in the hope that any lingering psychological leftovers would be resolved.

After a few minutes my initial outpouring of emotions settled down as I looked up through the trees to the blue sky. I'd seen that patch before, it was a strange feeling of the total recognition of one square of sky and I could hear myself repeating again and again, *"that's my piece of sky, its nowhere else, just here"*. That spot felt familiar to me. When I landed, I had lain here, focusing on the blue sky, willing the ambulance to come, and hoping above all that I would survive the next few minutes, hours, days and live.

Ella had come into the clearing behind me. When I turned around and saw her there, for a split second, I didn't recognise her. She didn't belong here in my memory; she hadn't been born. She just seemed totally out of place, watching me, and taking the whole event in. It felt strange to be able to show her the exact spot where I landed, where

I was carried out, and tell her all the details I could remember, how those there had reacted, what they had said, what I had thought and what her father had done. I was telling her this for the first time, in fact, apart from those who had been there, she was the only other person who had heard the detail of that few minutes in time or stood in that spot.

As I took in the scene and then looked across at her, I was filled with an immense feeling of gratitude and love. I was overwhelmed, I had survived and lived a full life without major life-changing injuries. If I had died, she wouldn't have been here at all, wouldn't have lived and grown into the wonderful, beautiful person she is today.

I had seen enough, wiped out by what I had experienced and the intensity of the emotions I had felt. As I had my final look around, we struggled to retrace our steps back to the runway, and Joe. My final thoughts were of how much I would love to be able to go back in time, lift myself up, give me a massive hug and tell me that everything was going to be alright, I wasn't going to die, I was going to have a good life, predictably unpredictable, and never boring.

When I came out from the clearing, I came out a different person. The whole experience had left me with a feeling of deep understanding and thankfulness. I had been lucky and whatever reason that was for, I had survived where others wouldn't have, and that clarity was enough to take into the future and begin the hard work of moving on.

We all arrived home, deep in our own thoughts after that first visit and, over the next few days, I thought of nothing else. I felt a mixture of emotions as I began to piece together how the accident had impacted on my life. *Would I have made the same choices and decisions anyway, or did my experience shape my future, make me a better person, or influence the career choices I later made?* I know it did, but to what extent I will never know.

It feels strange now that, even though I wanted answers, especially to explain what was happening in my mind and my NDE, I hadn't spent any time over the years pouring over books where experts explained trauma and near-death experiences, or to read stories of people who had been in similar situations. Usually this would be my "go to place", my comfort zone. If I didn't understand something I would study it widely until I knew as much as I could. Much of my life has been steeped an academia, referencing every sentence, my views had to be backed up by evidence and marked as valid by somebody else and in the end, I lost my own voice and confidence in my own opinion. This time was different and liberating. I realised that I was the "expert" on my own experience, my views mattered, and I wouldn't need to study or rely on others' knowledge to know what trauma and all that goes with it feels like and the harm, but also strength, it gives.

That need to find an explanation for the events of the accident, and the need to talk to someone who understood had become stifled for a myriad of reasons; the perceptions of others, the obvious disbelief in what I was telling them, their persistent need to share how the accident had impacted them, my initial desire to hide what had actually happened, and more importantly, my need to protect others as much as myself and shield them from thinking about such an horrific event. So, I completely ignored the psychological effects as much as I could, concentrating on my physical recovery, as this was much easier to get to grips with and something that others could see and then understand. Going back changed all that, the memory became a reality. It was as if I had been brought back to the time immediately after the accident, when that curiosity and hunger for knowledge was there, all the excuses I had used to avoid knowing were not relevant anymore.

The return opened up a whole new world for me, and a potentially exciting future where I could do something useful with the whole experience, both for myself to move on positively, and hopefully to let others know it is possible to bounce back when you need to. I wanted to press the unmute button, to set the record straight, capture the entwined experiences both Joe and I had, and finally commit it to paper.

I asked Ella how the visit to Bishopscourt had made her feel, I wanted to know what she had thought and what it was like for her to now see the place where the accident had happened and if it had changed how she felt about the stories she had heard over the years. A couple of days later she sent me a text, that I will never forget and that she has given me permission to share with you.

Ella's Experience

"Visiting the small patch of forest that saved my Mum's life was a very profound moment for me. Taking in the surroundings and seeing the stretches of concrete that surrounded the place where she landed, made me understand the true miracle that took place 25 years ago. Walking into the forest filled me with a mixture of anxiety and awe. I was in awe of my mum's strength and courage to go to a place that inflicted so much pain on her, both mentally and physically. Surprisingly I saw so much beauty in the patch of the forest where we stood, showing how out

of place I was from the event that had unfolded there. The grass and undergrowth were bright green, it smelled like summer flowers and wetness and the sun was peacefully beating down through a large opening in the treetops. I could only imagine my mum lying there 25 years ago and my dad, among other people, chaotically rushing to her in fear for her life.

I saw so much beauty and strength in my mum the day we returned to that place, which made me proud to be her daughter, thankful she survived and forever grateful for her ability to turn something ugly into something inspiring. When I was leaving the trees, I spotted my dad standing beyond the perimeter of the grass.

My mum pointed out the bottom of the runway, which was beside the trees. She told me that was where dad had first told her he loved her. My dad's eyes lit up and they smiled together, perfectly encompassing the moral of this story.

In a place that caused them both so much pain, there was also a hell of a lot of love. God gave my mum the gift of life that day, which she later passed onto me and for that I will always be grateful."

Act Two

So ... What Happened?

"When you try your best but you don't succeed

... Lights will guide you home

And ignite your bones

And I will try to fix you ..."

- **Fix You - Coldplay**

Chapter Three

Ground rush is Scary

The day of the accident was a beautifully crisp still day, quite warm for April, and there was a definite smell of Spring in the air. No clouds, no wind, it was perfect for jumping. The clocks had just gone forward for Spring, and it felt like we were all coming out of hibernation and back to life after many short winter days at the parachute centre; hanging around, waiting for the clouds to lift, the rain to stop, or the wind to drop. I have always loved that time of the year, when the days begin to lengthen, the sunrise is earlier and the evenings are stretching out, rather than going out to work in the dark and coming home in the dark, not wanting to go out again. Skydiving becomes more predictable as the weather gets better on that day there was a buzz of enthusiasm and busyness around the drop zone.

Over the previous winter months, the weather had been bad, and days were short, so it was great to get a decent day to jump. I hadn't been able to consistently jump as my weekends were full and the boys were not seeing their father as often then, I didn't have time on my own. I loved just staying at home at weekends with the kids as I worked 5 days per week, which were brilliant hours for a nurse but money was tight and spending it on jumping wasn't a priority.

I had no intention of jumping that day, which was unusual for me as I was normally fighting to get my name on the list to go first in order to be able to pack more jumps in on one day. In fact, I hadn't jumped over the Winter very often and wasn't in the right mindset just then, it didn't feel right, an uneasy feeling in the pit of my stomach, a dread, sense of foreboding, intuition, or maybe a subconscious warning. I couldn't put my finger on what was wrong, but everything in me was telling me not to do it.

Over the few weeks before the accident I had a definite uneasy, ominous feeling about jumping but could not put a finger on why. I remember vividly that I wasn't sleeping well as I was having a recurrent dream that a car was chasing me through trees at high speed, trying to hit me. I couldn't make out the driver, just a black shadow. I had to run faster, so fast I knew I would stop at any time, unable to carry on. The panic and fear were intense. As the car reached me, I would jump out of the way onto the verge, or run to a tree, the branches appearing to reach out to welcome me and then hold me and keep me safe. In my dream, when I got there,

I could feel the overwhelming relief that I had outrun the car and thinking, *"See? You didn't get me this time"*, as it shot past me, disappearing down the road and out of sight. It was terrifying, waking me up each time in a cold sweat, heart pounding and my legs physically ached the next day for no reason at all.

I know that there may be those who would say, "hindsight's a wonderful thing," and I would have too, and not linked it to any type of premonition if it hadn't been for the return of the dream immediately after the accident. This time it was just me and the car, there were no safe trees and no verge to jump onto to escape, only the path, the width of the car, and no escape. I couldn't run fast enough, and the car hit me time and time again and there was a voice saying, *"well, I hit you now"*. I was always trying to get out of the dream, but I couldn't wake up. For me it is easy to link this to my feelings of reservation, another piece of the jigsaw, leading up to the perfect storm.

The pressure of trying to get the skydiving manoeuvres right on each jump was beginning to spoil the experience and I was wondering if it was time to stop. I couldn't understand why I seemed to move forward and do a perfectly good jump to move to the next step, and then took a step back messing up the next jump. I was often being "put back on the rope", the static line, like a baby in a harness, until it became a standing joke as I became the "yoyo" of the club.

It was like my body detached from my head and just did its own thing. I was only a few good jumps away from achieving Category 8 level and this would mean I could jump with others and be given more freedom to jump as I wanted. The other students who were at the same stage as myself, and had also become part of the club, continued jumping whenever they could over the Winter and were bypassing me quickly, being as competitive as I was, I was determined to catch them up. Progressing up the categories was exhilarating though, with every jump bringing a new experience, a new perspective, new challenge, and more and more enjoyment. To be able to get it right and work out why, was brilliant and made you just feel on top of the world, accomplishing something special, feeling strong and in control. There were those who seemed to take naturally to skydiving with perfect body positions, perfect openings and, of course, perfect landings. And then there were others, like me, who took a bit longer to master the craft.

Then there was Joe. I'm sure anyone who has a boyfriend as a teacher or instructor will relate to me when I say combining the two is a recipe for disaster. Critiques became pillow talk, and I wasn't consistently good which led to disagreements and frustration as Joe couldn't understand why I was just not concentrating. He used to say that when he was teaching me a new move, he would see my eyes glaze over and he knew he'd lost me from the start. Doing what I was told was never a strong point. This would infuriate Joe who was a naturally great skydiver, and seriously dedicated to the sport. I was jumping for pleasure but as with all aspects of my life I wanted perfection, this seemed to elude me in skydiving. This was one of the reasons we agreed that I would only jump with other instructors, so these two parts of our lives would remain separate and if we had just stuck with this arrangement there is no doubt that the accident would not have happened.

The boys were with me that day as I wasn't going to jump, and the weather was good we decided to go on a day out and then to pick Joe up after the course he was instructing. We had decided that this was another reason we wouldn't jump together, if the boys were with us, one would always stay on the ground, as they were always up to something and in case something went wrong. Neither of us thought it would. There is a small beach at Ballyhornan that was never very busy where we could watch the plane and those jumping, I packed a picnic and set off for precious time as a family. I could see by the number of plane lifts how busy the day at the club had been, I left it until late in the afternoon before going there to collect Joe.

When I arrived, the students had all got to jump and this added to the excitement I could feel as soon as I got there. There were a few students left, maybe doing a second jump, or progressing to freefall and the final lift of the day was being planned. One of the student skydivers really wanted to go up as he had completed three good static line jumps and only had a twenty-four-hour window to try his first freefall, and one of our close friends also wanted to jump as he was working his way up the categories, just as I was. The plane would not take off unless there were enough jumpers to fill it and I was the only one left who could use the last slot. Again, I had reservations as Joe was the only instructor available and that meant we would both be in the air at the same time, and we had agreed jumping together was not a good option.

I felt pressured to jump, I hadn't planned it and really didn't want to, but I knew the frustration at this stage in skydiving when you just wanted to move on to the next level, I couldn't refuse. Our friends offered to keep an eye on the boys who were playing outside and watching the plane, I knew they would be in safe hands. I was also acutely aware of my feelings of dread and my heart just wasn't in it, but I finally caved in and got kitted up, watched as safety checks were carried out on my kit and practiced a few practice runs through the turn manoeuvre I would be trying.

I was to do a 360-degree turn and I followed what I thought was the normal instruction for those of us who were jumping at this level, where the instructors would tell us to do a turn and if we did it well to look at our altimeter to check our height and if we were high enough, then we would do another 360-degree turn in the opposite direction. This would become a major bone of contention afterwards every time Joe and I talked about what had gone wrong after the accident. Joe had told me to do "a" 360-degree turn, meaning I should do only one.

As a result of not being able to jump consistently I felt like I was continually starting from scratch at each level I tried to achieve, and on this occasion, it was these turns I was struggling with. This was my second try and I had not been in the right body position before, had dropped my arm too low and spun and was not in the right position when I opened my chute.

Joe and I agreed that he would come out of the plane after me, watch what I was doing and give me an aerial critique so he could see what the problem was if I fell off the move. I was to pick a focus point on the horizon, drop my arm, slightly, and turn slowly until I returned to the focus point, therefore a complete 360-degree turn. Well, that was the plan.

As an extra precaution all student kits had an activating device that would fire my reserve at a certain height and speed if, for whatever reason, I couldn't do this myself. My device was set at 1400 feet and was still designed to work when the main parachute was opened at around the same height and speed. The height and speed I was at when I opened my main parachute during the fall was another main contributor to the series of events that followed.

I was rehearsing the jump in my mind as we got into the plane and on the way up, calming myself and focusing on what I was to do as a way of ignoring any other feelings going on in my mind. I was determined this would be the perfect jump.

It's hard to describe what it's like as you're walking towards the plane, all kitted up and ready to go. It was a mix of excitement and trepidation, but excitement was always the overriding emotion. As soon as the kit went on, double layers of clothes under your jumpsuit, helmet with a one-way radio and the all-important gloves to stop fingers sticking to the strut as you left the plane, there was no going back. All the safety checks were done, I was safe, ready to go as I reassured myself that after 64 jumps, I would be fine, wouldn't I? Joe, the best instructor, and the man I trusted implicitly, would be there in the air with me to save me if something went wrong. It never crossed my mind that no-one would be able to on this jump.

That false feeling of safety was sold by everyone involved, which was totally bizarre as of course it is dangerous, and when accidents happened, they usually weren't a little bump or bruise, they were a torn ligament, broken bones, or something equally as serious. Although you practiced safety and reserve drills, careful packing of the parachute by an experienced person, double checks of your kit and trust in your instructors, it was never going to prepare you for more than the most common problems you may encounter, and never the ones you just couldn't get out of. These possibilities were just too scary to contemplate and the masquerade that we were just going for a walk in the park on the outside and being so scared on the inside became the norm. It wasn't that I didn't feel fear, I just learned to get into such a calm state that I would never run from the danger. The "fight, flight and freeze" reaction was so suppressed that I just didn't acknowledge it at all. I learned how to do this so well I even replaced the natural response with a feeling of extreme enjoyment and control, I freaked out any instructor I had when I left the step because of the genuine smile and lack of fear I appeared to have as I let go of the strut and fell backwards into the sky.

This control takes time and quite a few jumps to master, and it was always morbidly amusing for more experienced jumpers, when you got to the stage you had conquered, or suppressed, seeing first-time jumpers who regretted the choice of using skydiving as a way of being sponsored for charities leave the plane. There were many times that fear took over completely for these poor unsuspecting souls, who were "helped" to leave the step, but only remember experiencing elation when the parachute opens above their head, and they land safely. It is a bit like childbirth, when you forget the pain and memories of the exact events, and carry on having more children, thanking those you helped you and leaving your partner dumbfounded after hurling abuse at him, with no hope of a repeat and very sore hands, or when you pay a personal instructor to cause you pain under the guise of "keeping you fit and helping your mental health".

None of the students seemed to remember their fingers being peeled off the strut to let the slipstream take control and blow them off, or a gentle push by a kind-hearted instructor who just knew how much they would enjoy the experience and tell the story for years afterwards. In reality, it would have been far more dangerous to get back into the plane, as coming in from a step when the static line is attached to the inside of the plane on a hook under the pilot's seat, if the person slipped, or the line got caught, the parachute would start to open with the person still on the step or in the plane. The result could stall the plane and it would literally fall out of the sky and kill all on board or fill the plane with the parachute, with the same outcome. More importantly, for the jumpers who wanted to get out, the student would never be forgiven.

One such person, who wouldn't get off the step and was a friend of mine at the time, was so eager to impress the men at the club that rather than experience a jump, she decided to train, and go out on her own for a static-line jump. We were all a bit dubious, and I did warn her it was a bit of an extreme way to get attention, but she wanted to go ahead anyway. When she got out on the step she just wouldn't let go and Joe tried to peel her fingers off the strut, but it was like she was playing a piano as she put them back on every time. The plane began to tilt to one side. We found it hilarious afterwards, but at the time it wasn't amusing for anyone inside the plane. Those on board were used to students doing this, but after a few minutes it was just getting scary. The pilot had to do another circuit with her still on the step and even the slipstream that caused was not enough to blow her off. She was shouting so loudly that everyone on the ground could hear her screaming from 2,500 feet in the air. The trust that Joe, as the instructor had built up during the day stuck fast and when Joe said he would bring her back in she reached over to grab his hands at which point he "gently" let go of her, she finally fell off the step and we could all breathe a sigh of relief.

That day as the four of us walked to the plane on the runway, it was stuttering to life, with a blast of aviation fuel, an unforgettable smell and one I will always associate with skydiving. My heart was pounding, no light steps that day, instead the heavy, dragging feet I would imagine you would have if you were walking to a scaffold, praying that the sun would set more quickly and leave us with no choice but to cancel the flight.

I crawled into the plane and sat beside the pilot as I would be the last one to jump at the highest altitude. There was always silence as the plane lifted off the runway, all on board hoping it would take off properly and that nothing else could spoil our jump, the point of no return. I looked out the window at the points on the ground as they got smaller and smaller, the familiar places that orientated you in freefall and navigated you back to the drop zone. The village of Ballyhornan, the house with the right-angled roof, the Mourne Mountains, purple in the distance, the sea, and farmers' fields.

The plane had no door, there was always a blast of freezing air preparing you for how cold it would be outside and the instructor looking at the ground, directing the pilot to the best place to let us out so we would land near to the clubhouse.

The plane circled, gaining height, 1,000 feet, 2000 feet, 3,500 feet and as the plane straightened up, flying in a straight line, on the "run-in" the instruction was given to "cut" and the pilot reduced the engine's speed to slow down and let the student get out without being blown away by the slipstream. It was as though the plane had stopped completely and was drifting across the sky, revving up again only when the jumper had gone. The instructor would then shout "feet-out" at the student, a signal to climb out onto the step under the wing and grab the strut. I could only imagine their heart beating out of their chest and their stomach in their mouth as they struggled to manoeuvre out to the open door. Looking in at the instructor you waited for the final command *"gooooo"* as you let go and fell backwards.

The same happened again at 5,000 feet to let the next jumper go and I knew that in a couple of minutes it would be my turn. My adrenalin and excitement were building, all the misgivings forgotten as the calm kicked in and I was ready to go. The plane came to 6,500 feet, straightened for the "run in" and I moved to the open doorway with Joe behind me. The anticipation was extreme as I looked out of the door and down to the ground to get my bearings before I left the plane. Joe gave the usual instructions and I got out of the plane onto the step, holding onto the strut. It was absolutely freezing as the icy slipstream caught my breath and I fell backwards from the plane.

I began the 360-degree turn after around 8 seconds, before coming face to face with the ground. I looked around for the point I had picked to be the static point, I would know when I saw it again that I had completed the turn successfully. I had picked Slieve Donard, the tallest peak in the Mourne mountains and 15 miles away, as it was clear that evening and the full range of the mountains looked beautiful. I checked my altimeter and dropped my right arm to begin the turn. It went well, I had turned 360-degrees faultlessly, returning to my focus point and when I rechecked my altimeter, I was at 4,500ft, facing earth and I knew I had enough height for a second try. This time I dropped my left arm and as I moved around, I decided to test out if I could stop and start again when I wanted by moving my arm ever so slightly up and down. Everything was going brilliantly, and I felt in control the whole time where I hadn't been before.

As I came around again to see Slieve Donard, Joe was there instead, close to me, with a giant smile and thumbs up in congratulations. It was unexpected, but I was happy he was there and in that second, I knew I had nailed it. The perfect jump.

I had never seen anyone's face in free-fall, it was fascinating seeing the effect of terminal velocity on his face, his skin rippling and sunken and in the same body position as me. We seemed suspended in time, both travelling at the same speed, losing height with every second that passed, but with no feeling of this. I had completely lost altitude awareness. I focused on Joe without considering how fast we were falling. I could see him check his altimeter and watched as his smile disappeared, replaced by the fear and panic on his face as he tried to signal to warn me how low we were going, but I didn't understand the frantic signals he was making for me to open my chute as I hadn't seen them before. I was confused as he tried to get closer, trying to get to my handle and pull it, but he kept sliding backwards, unable to reach me. When he couldn't, the only thing that he hoped would jolt me back to reality was for him to open his chute in the hope that I would realise how low we were and pull mine. He opened and stopped, suspended until his parachute inflated, I continued to fall, glancing at my altimeter. The needle was rapidly moving to the red zone, to 1400ft, 8 seconds to impact and I was in shock at how low I was. Immediately I was grappling to find my handle, in total panic but at last it was in my hand, and I was pulling it as hard as I could. Instantly I felt the familiar tug of the parachute opening and the feeling of relief was overwhelming … I had escaped. I was very low but would make it back alive to a telling-off from Joe, barred from jumping for a few weeks, but at least alive.

Suddenly, I felt an unexpected second jolt and as I looked up in horror, I could see the white canopy of my reserve parachute shooting up into my purple and blue main one, like a firework shooting into the sky before it explodes.

I watched in slow motion as it went straight up into the centre of my main canopy that still hadn't had the time to properly inflate before the reserve parachute hit, collapsing the main one around it. It looked like a bundle of washing, a rainbow of blue, purple, and white lines everywhere. I remember watching for what seemed like forever, willing one of them to inflate, thinking to myself, *"they never taught us how to get out of this one"*, *"please, please open…I don't know what to do."* But neither one did.

That was when I realised how serious this was and how much crap I was actually in. The realisation that my life would be over in seconds hit me like a knock-out punch, that sinking feeling from my head to my toes and a sense of impending doom. I was in a frenzy, knowing I had only seconds to solve the unsolvable problem, thinking of as many ways as I could to do something to save myself, anything, still hoping I had a chance to survive as the alternative was certain to be death. My first instinct was to try to "cut away" my main canopy from my reserve. This drill had been implanted in my brain and practiced before every jump in case the main canopy malfunctioned. In this case I knew I couldn't, the lines from both were too entangled and *what if I made the situation worse? ...* as if that was possible. I tried to work out which lines belonged to which canopy, but it wasn't possible, so that wasn't an option. The toggles and lines of both the main and reserve parachutes were the same colour, I had no way to distinguish and separate them. I began to speed up again and be thrown violently round and round, my feet were horizontal to my body and the lines from the canopy were twisting to the back of my head, lifting my harness up to my neck, threatening to strangle me. I can still remember the panic, the type that spreads pins and needles all over your body and makes you feel physically sick.

I had no options left, but to resign myself to the certain fact that I was going to die. I could hear myself plead for my life over and over again, to God, or a higher being, bargaining to change my ways, if only I got the chance. I was thinking over and over, *"I'm too young for this, the boys will have no one, this is not happening right now, I'm not dying today!"* The pleading meant nothing, all my chances for a late reprieve were gone and I was completely on my own. An intense feeling of loneliness and hopelessness engulfed me that I hope I will never feel again.

Thoughts and memories were whizzing by, leaving my mind as if I was looking at snapshots in a photo-album, turning the pages over at break-neck speed, of events that had happened to me, pictures of loved ones and friends, memories, conversations, regrets, happiness ... an immediate life review that I hadn't expected and wasn't ready to have. The review was over, my mind was now empty. I was left with the boys, their faces smiling up at me and the soft warm smell of them snuggling into me when they climbed into my bed in the mornings was so strong that even in this situation of total horror there was also an overwhelming feeling of utter love and a longing for them that was all-encompassing.

Afterwards, when I think of this part of the experience, it feels surreal, and I can never describe in words what that level of terror is really like. I now know I had blocked out further memories of those following few seconds; to lessen the feelings and try to forget, missing out the parts that were the most traumatic, unable to fathom the enormity of how horrific it really was, like skipping a chapter of a book, until I got to the more comforting parts. The brain is fantastic at protecting you, but trauma can play tricks on you and regardless of the years that pass it can re-emerge to overtake your mind without warning, something I would find out for myself as I worked on this book and opened Pandora's Box.

In less than a split second the terror and frenzy were gone along with the negative thoughts, and as with so many words in this story, words can't convey the reality, and the ultimate calm and tranquillity that I felt next. Imagine every earthly worry just disappears, all the bills, responsibilities, demands, and expectations are gone, they are not relevant to the here and now. What is left is a stripped-down version of yourself, just you, an in-depth insight into what is important in your life, like being in a timeless, floating bubble, giving me time to think like never before.

The strangest sensation followed; one I can remember today as clearly as when I experienced it. I could feel myself being lifted up by the shoulders, sliding out of my human body, as if my soul was pulled out of me in the blink of an eye, my body no longer needed. It was painless and comfortable, not like the tightness of the lines at the back of my neck or the harness digging into my inner thighs. I felt safe, like someone was holding on to me, lifting me out of the horror, carrying me upwards. The feelings were tinged with an intense feeling of longing, desperate to stay but wanting to go at the same time, being sucked away from my life.

I could see my malfunctioned canopy in a bundle, with its lines over the top canopy, as I looked down from my vantage point and could describe this clearly after the accident. The same view that Joe would later tell me about. My friends on the ground were running, I could see them scattering, like a herd of animals running outwards, away from a hunting lion. The plane was coming into land, and someone was waving to the pilot, probably warning him not to land yet in case I hit the runway. In the background Joe was screaming my name, ruining my peace and quiet and I remember thinking, *"would you ever shut up, you're spoiling this."*

It was surreal, as I looked down, calm and contented, wondering why they were bothering to panic, it was senseless, I was gone. I was disconnecting from the scene, separating from my life. I was in a middle place, knowing I was not on earth but in transition to somewhere else, still conscious, and alive, not in my body and no longer scared, looking down at others and wanting to tell them, *"It's ok, don't worry, there's nothing you can do, I'm not under that canopy, I'm already gone".*

And then I seemed to travel further, somewhere else, I was in another place that made perfect sense to me and where I totally belonged.

I felt like the whole scene was encased in a snow-globe and I was inside. The sky arched over my head, a colour of blue so deep I didn't recognize it as our earthly blue sky. I was in a clearing, in long grass up to my waist and every type of wildflower you could imagine. There was a path leading to the horizon with beautiful sunset colours and another path leading in the opposite direction. I knew I had walked along this path to the place I now stood. Not walked in steps, but with a sensation of moving, getting there, floating, weightless without a human body. The colours of the sun, the flowers and grass were amazing, so vibrant, unnaturally deep, but bright at the same time. I could name the colours, but at the same time it was a version of them I had never seen before, or since. The place I was in reminded me of childhood memories of hiding in fields beside our house in the country when the grass was tall no one could see me and I could hide from everyone and get lost in my own thoughts, watching the sky, surrounded by ladybirds and bugs climbing up the stems.

There were strong smells of freshly cut grass and the scents of the flowers Everything was quiet, still, peaceful, and so, so calm. I felt weightless and couldn't feel or see my body, no wind rushing by no concept of falling and time didn't mean anything. I could have stayed there forever. A beautiful feeling of peace enveloped me as I handed everything in my life over to be taken care of by something unknown, but that I could trust completely. I was in a much, much bigger place than the earth, the universe and more than just a tiny, insignificant little person or some a dot on a page in the grand scheme of things.

I felt a strong presence around me, giving me a definite choice of whether to live or die, the biggest one of my life, a dilemma, terrifying in case I made the wrong one, but knowing there was no-one else but me who could decide. At the same time, I immediately knew what I wanted for the first time in my life. I trusted my decision completely. I could start walking to the horizon or turn round and travel back down the path that I was sure would end up back in my normal life. It could have been luck, fate, God saving me or *"just not my time"*. I wanted the boys to know how much they were loved and wanted, I wanted to tell them one more time, and many after that. I couldn't leave them, they needed me.

Those thoughts overtook the want to stay and immediately I was re-entering my body, like putting my hand into a glove and I felt my own senses again, able to see through my eyes, feeling the weight of my body under the canopy and back into reality. Intense fear and panic grabbed me again, like I had woken up from a dream to a horrendous nightmare. I was immediately back to being thrown violently around and I could see I was hurtling towards small trees and bushes, I rolled up into a ball as much as I could, covering my face with my hands. I thought I would impale on the bushes or land on the runway, but either way

I was going to die. The speed I was falling at was incredible, I felt like I was back at terminal velocity.

Ground rush is so scary, the green ground was swirling up to grab me, I was going fast, plummeting like a stone. I couldn't breathe as I tried to pull my feet back up to avoid what was happening, away from the ground rush to avoid hitting the ground, but that was never going to work. I braced myself. The last thoughts I remember, before I hit the ground were *"shit, this is really going to hurt"*.

Smashing into the earth at that speed was like an electric shock, or a massive wave coming from the ground into my feet upwards through my body and out of my head. I just seemed to crumple, shattering like glass, the splinters held inside my skin as I landed first on my left side. I could hear my bones cracking down this side of my body and my teeth and jaw crushing, like the sound of metal in a car crusher. I felt lines opening from my chin to my forehead, like upward tickles and my jaw felt it had moved up into my nose. As soon as I hit the ground I was back up in the air and fell onto my back beside bushes. The last part to hit was the back of my head and I could hear the thump of my helmet on the ground when I finally came to rest.

I didn't feel pain to begin with, I was winded and stunned, but that was it. In the seconds before the pain kicked in, I lay on my back looking up at the clear sky as it dawned on me that I was still alive. I could smell grass and soil around me, in a body-sized hole I had made for myself in the ground. All I could think was, *"what just happened, where have I been?"*

It's ridiculous the things you think of and what you remember from a time like this. My immediate thought was, *"wow, how great was that? I got it right, I've survived, that was the ultimate high, the best jump I've ever done".* I knew I would never get that good a buzz again.

I could see Joe spiralling hard, desperate to land and thought, *"he's going to kill himself if he keeps doing that."* In a sick, sick moment I said to myself, *"if I played dead, I wonder what he would do".*

Then the pain kicked in … it was extreme. I could see my left leg was at a strange angle on the ground, the pain like an intense cramp that never goes, and I thought it was still up in the air, needing to be straightened. Afterwards I learned that my left leg had fractured upwards, with one piece of thigh bone moving beside the other.

My mouth was continually filling with blood and broken teeth, which I tried not to swallow and to spit out, coughing out blood and making my face looking dramatically more injured than it was. At the time those who found me were imagining the worst. The strap holding my helmet on was digging into my face, but I couldn't open the catch and knew it was supporting my chin, probably a good thing as I had broken many bones in my face.

It is at a time like this when being a nurse isn't helpful. I knew too much and began to diagnose my injuries, but as bad as the pain was, it was a good sign, I wasn't paralysed. The most terrifying part was not knowing what other injuries I had that weren't obvious. If I had internal injuries, I was aware of the risk to life that damage to any organ could lead to.

"What if I had survived the landing which was amazing enough, having chosen to live, but then aspirate on teeth and blood, choking? That would suck. Maybe someone would take my helmet off and paralyse me, would I get to a hospital quickly enough to save my life?"

I saw Joe first as he came through the bushes, but he seemed to freeze, rooted to the spot as soon as he saw me, his face etched with fear and panic and astonishment that I was still breathing, trying to talk, conscious and very much alive. I was screaming, pleading for someone to take the pain away and make it stop. I could hear others coming, pushing past Joe and remember seeing their reactions, a mixture of shock and horror. They have since told me they thought they were going to find a body, but to see me still alive, screaming, blood everywhere, my face and leg a strange shape was terrifying as they realised, I needed emergency help. One guy threw up over my boots, my favourite leather jumping boots, and my jumpsuit. I was thinking, *"what are you doing? I'll have to get them cleaned now"*, never thinking that I would have to have them cut off, with the rest of my clothes, when I got to the hospital.

I was willing myself to go into shock, to lose consciousness and get out of the situation and pain I was in. At one stage my goggles, still on my face, steamed up and I thought that at last shock had kicked in and I would fade into unconsciousness soon. Imagine my disappointment when one of our friends wiped them clear and I realised that wasn't the case. No matter how awful the situation there was still humour and looking back this is one of many more amusing memories that have stayed with me and with others who were there.

One of the girls was holding my hand and telling me I'd be alright and that was what I clung to until the paramedics arrived. After the initial frenzy, everyone around me was quiet, they had done all they could, except wait until help arrived. It was like my voice was in the distance, echoing in the silence as I carried on screaming.

There was no amount of drugs that would have taken the pain away at that time, but I've never been so glad to get as much as they could give me without killing me. I was trying to explain my injuries, but just couldn't speak clearly enough and the combination of shock, adrenaline and fear kept me alert at the time, helping me to focus on what I thought they should be doing, in my head thinking, *"put in a needle, get a drip up, put me on a monitor, keep me topped up with the good stuff and get me out of here!"*

A good friend of ours, the skydiver who had got out of the plane before me, recalled his version of events about the treatment I got. He remembers the paramedic realising my wrist was broken, but only when he stood on it and that he was terrified to take control of my head as I was lifted. My friend totally refused when he was asked to do it, as he knew he could never forgive himself if he caused me an injury that left me paralysed for the rest of my life; the paramedic had to do it.

After enough had been done to stabilise me at the accident site, the task of lifting me to get me through the bushes to the ambulance was the next hurdle and I realised that meant having to be moved and be lifted onto a stretcher, it was agonising as everyone tried to carry me without falling over stones and the rough terrain yet going as fast as they could to get me into the ambulance. I remember wishing I had gone on a diet and apologising for being heavy. It really didn't dawn on me that that was the least of my worries just then.

Joe was able to come in the ambulance with me and the boys were taken away by friends. My oldest boy was watching the plane, waiting for me to jump out and saw me plummet to earth. In all the chaos and urgent action that needed to happen no one thought to explain what had happened and tell him that I was alright. It must have been terrifying for him when he realised it was me, he saw falling, and didn't know whether I was still alive. That is a memory I can't erase from his mind, and I will be forever sorry for that.

The trip to the closest hospital along narrow, windy country roads seemed to last forever. I had been topped up with so much pain relief and was sucking so hard on gas and air it would have been enough to knock an elephant out, but

I was still awake and now floating in a lovely haze of the best cocktail imaginable. Afterwards, Joe told me I kept saying, *"if this is heaven, I think I'll stay here"* over and over, but as the paramedic leaned over me to check my vital signs, I saw nothing but concern.

Every time we came to a bend in the road, I felt the break in my leg separate. When we got to the local hospital the entrance was on a downward slope, I felt as if my leg had completely disconnected and was already inside as I was wheeled in. The accident department seemed quite empty, and I was brought into the treatment room immediately. I still didn't realise that this would happen so fast and that I had life threatening injuries. I could hear myself screaming, cursing, and then apologising every time I was moved, and I imagine everyone in the hospital could hear too. My clothes were cut off, X-rays had to be taken, a splint put on my leg and my arm and there was a feeling of urgency and seriousness all around me.

It's hard to explain how scary and vulnerable it is to be a patient in this situation and certainly something I didn't appreciate as a nurse. My ears were blocked from the speed at which I had descended, but I could still partially hear and see all that was going on around me. The staff discussing my injuries and what would happen next in hushed tones, the X-ray on the lightbox showing the fracture in all its glory and needles and tubes being stuck into me from every angle. I knew saving my life was obviously the main priority, but it was the little things that counted most. Someone holding my hand and telling me not to be scared, that I was going to be alright, covering me up when my clothes were being cut off and explaining what was going on was vital and was probably more important to me than anything else at that moment in time. No one I knew was in the room with me while I was being treated and although I understand this, I wish it could have been someone I knew and loved to do the handholding and give the reassurance.

Joe came in as soon as he could. He looked worried, upset, but I just wanted to hug him and cling onto him forever. It was the first time we had spoken to each other in private. He was telling me, *"I love you; you're going to be*

OK, and I'll see you as soon as I can. I'll make sure the boys are OK and let your parents know what has happened."

If I ever had any doubts about how much he cared for me, or how much I loved him, they vanished in that moment.

I was moved to the Royal Victoria Hospital, with regional facilities and specialist trauma care as soon as I could be transferred. I don't remember that journey until I was wheeled into the resuscitation area on the trolley. I felt out of my body again, but not as vividly as before, seeing myself below like a Queen Bee with a swarm of drones around me. They were many staff around, someone obviously in charge giving orders and others connecting me to a monitor, fixing my drips, putting up blood, checking me over from top to toe, doing observations and rushing to get equipment. It was like a manic flurry of activity, but also a well-oiled engine, rehearsed with skill and efficiency and while they were there, I had confidence they knew what they were doing.

Was I really that seriously damaged? I felt that I wasn't quite there, like I was watching an episode of a medical drama, not believing it was me lying there. As long as they didn't roll in the crash trolley, I'd be fine. After a while fewer staff seemed to be with me, like the calm after the storm, my condition had stabilised and to me, in my drugged-out state, they only came to do observations. I felt alone, scared and hadn't a clue how seriously ill I was, or the extent of my injuries. I knew the sudden stop at over 100mph, should have told me that my body really wasn't designed for that level of impact. There were no decelerators like seat belts or airbags, or the frame of a car to slow me down. I hit the ground so fast that there were bound to be major injuries, all the possibilities were spinning around in my head as I drifted in and out of consciousness.

I lay looking up at the florescent strip lightning for what seemed like hours, listening to the monitor beeps and the noises of the Emergency Department and I was terrified, scared that I would be forgotten about and die without anyone noticing. I think I reverted to my childhood and remember wanting my mum and dad for some comfort and reassurance. I wondered how Joe would break this news to them and how they would react, the telephone ringing in the middle of the night would tell them it was something serious before they even reached it, but as my next of kin, it couldn't wait until morning in case they were needed. Staff came and went to do essentials, but I wanted someone to tell me I was going to survive, even if they didn't think I would, to explain the injuries I had and how they would be fixed. I hadn't thought my injuries were so serious that I would need to go straight to theatre but then how would they not be after impacting from such a height and speed. I watched the number of pints of blood being used and still it didn't dawn on me.

I was working in the Royal at this time and when I was wheeled into the theatre's anaesthetic room, I knew the staff there. I had been working with them earlier that week, they were obviously shocked it was me who needed the emergency operation. I couldn't work out how they were going to anesthetise me as my mouth was such a mess and was exhausted thinking of all the possibilities. I watched as they prepared, getting ready to put me to sleep, so clinical, but casual at the same time, talking to each other about their weekends as if they hadn't a care in the world, it was just another day in the office, and I wished it was me nursing someone else and not being the one on the trolley. Suddenly, I was surrounded by surgeons discussing the operation and the multiple injuries they needed to fix, but I didn't want to hear ... I was thinking, *"just get on with it and let me go to sleep".*

Finally, finally they asked me to count backwards from ten to one as they covered my nose with a mask and began to inject the anaesthetic, not getting past eight as I drifted off into oblivion, unconscious at last.

Chapter Four

Joe's Story

Very soon after the accident and for the ensuing years, Joe's perspective was never heard by those around us, and he never really discussed how he had felt and the trauma he had experienced. To begin with he was shocked to the core to have been involved in an accident of this magnitude involving a person he loved, one he had been an integral part of and that caused him much guilt. The tale became an interesting story to tell over a few drinks, it became an experience that only happened to me and not Joe. But Joe and I are the only ones who really know what happened in freefall that day and how the last pieces of the jigsaw fell into place to cause the perfect storm, the accident that changed both our lives.

Twenty-five years later we still hadn't really discussed it fully. For some years talking about the actual events would lead to a row between us, me saying, *"if you hadn't come down in front of me this wouldn't have happened",* and Joe coming back with, *"well if you had just done what you were told…".*

They are painful memories of a time when we were both traumatised and trying to get through the repercussions of an event, we were both involved in, trying to cling on to what we had together, and I often wondered how we stayed together and how we could move on. I always saw the accident as a jigsaw with lots of pieces lining up to make it happen. I couldn't ignore the ominous sense of not wanting to jump, the recurring dream, the choice I had made during the NDE, to push back under the canopy and live. I had put the parachute on my back and the responsibility and risk I took was mine, and it was also my responsibility to get myself back on my feet and make my life happen again, albeit differently than I was expecting. He hadn't purposely gone out to hurt me in any way, I never blamed him for his small part in the events and I knew that we were going to be together for the rest of our lives so we would find a way to make it work. That wasn't the thing that would split us up, it wasn't important enough. Joe and I handled the aftermath differently, he had managed to pack his feelings up and put them as far in the back of his mind as he could and recalling them now has brought him mixed emotions but is also a chance to tell his side of the story.

Joe's Story

"I had gone down to the Club early that morning as there were many students booked in for a course and I would be instructing them. The weather was lovely and there was a good chance they would all get jumping at the end of the day. A course would take all day as there was so much practicing of safety procedures and landings. There was only one other instructor there that day, and in between lessons there were several plane lifts to take more experienced students up, and parachutes to be packed. Joanne had been at the beach with the boys and had come to pick me up as we weren't planning to stay overnight. The day had gone well, we were having a great time and there was a definite buzz around the drop zone. When Joanne came in, I was finishing lifts with the students that I had trained that day and they were then all leaving, but there was one guy who had just been cleared for his first freefall and our friend was to do a "20 second delay", but we were short one person. Joanne wasn't keen, she had the boys

there and we weren't to jump together, but I coaxed and persuaded her until she gave in.

We had time to practice on the "creeper" to get Joanne's body positions right, agree what we were going to do and what headings we were going to use. It was all very routine, putting on our kits, checking Joanne's before and after she put it on, and checking the height settings on the Automatic Activating Device (AAD) that would fire off the reserve parachute at a certain height and speed if she was in trouble and couldn't open normally. For that jump it was set for 1400 feet. I checked her again as we got to the plane, the ripcord and flaps were in place and her one-way radio was working in case she needed any guidance from the ground. The sun was sinking lower in the sky, beginning to turn the blue-sky purple, we had to take off quickly if we were to have enough light to jump safely.

The student who had needed to jump for his first freefall left the plane at 3,500 feet and did it perfectly. Normally there would be a celebration for him doing so well, the stocks would be out, and a few drinks involved, but he was forgotten about in the panic of what happened afterwards. The next altitude for the second jumper who left the plane was 5,000 feet. As he left, I was leaning out to watch him, and he opened at too low an altitude, which would have been a 'grounding' offence where he wouldn't have been allowed to jump for a time as a punishment had events not taken over. I remember thinking, "I'm going to have a word with him when I get down". The plane circled upwards to 6,500 feet and I called for the engine to be stalled for Joanne to get out and as she climbed onto the step she had her usual unnerving smile, face full of excitement, as she looked back in at me. As she let go of the strut and fell backwards, I counted for 3 seconds, jumped out after her and got into a seated position to watch what she was doing. She started her first turn at about 8 seconds, before she hit terminal velocity and became face to earth. When she finished, she was at 5,500 feet and it had gone perfectly. I was excited and happy for her; she had nailed it. I was in the seated position no further than 100 feet above her and I could see she was checking her height as we fell through

5,000 feet. I knew we had enough time before she opened at 3,500 feet and I made the fateful split-second decision to go down to her to congratulate her for the perfect turn, I changed my body position, swooping down ending up around 20 feet in front of her. This was the decision I have regretted ever since and that brought me so much guilt and regret afterwards. I would never have done this if we hadn't been in a relationship, being an instructor, I knew the risks, but in that moment, I put those aside.

As soon as I was in front of Joanne, she had begun a second turn, obviously realising when she checked her altimeter that she could fit a second turn in. This turn was a bit slower as she was moving her arm up and down to practice stopping and starting. It was clear that the penny had finally dropped that this is what she was meant to be doing. The second turn ended at around 3,500 feet, but I suddenly realised that I was close in front of her, in place of her heading, she would have been expecting to see the Mourne Mountains, and she wouldn't have seen anyone in freefall before. She was smiling at me when she first saw me, but then I could see the confusion spread over her face and I knew she had lost altitude awareness. I was desperately trying to get her to open, signalling frantically and pretending to open my chute but Joanne hadn't learnt the signals yet, I could see she didn't understand. This only took five or six seconds, and we were now going through 2,000 feet.

I tried to get to her to pull her parachute handle, but knew we were going far too low, the only thing I could do was open my chute and hope by doing this she would realise how low we were. I opened my parachute at 1700 feet and lost Joanne for a couple of seconds as my parachute opened. I looked down praying she had opened and when I saw her, she was around 500 feet below me with a canopy in a complete mess. I saw her reserve canopy opening into the main canopy and collapsing them both as it tangled, couldn't inflate and starting to rotate. My main thought was that she was going to die, there was no way she could get out of this, as I began to spiral down, thinking that if I could get down fast, I could wrap my legs into the canopy to slow her down, but I was on the verge of passing out trying to get down. I could hear myself screaming her name over and over and at that point she disappeared into the ground so fast, like a stone falling. I didn't see her hit the ground, or don't want to remember it if I did, as to see someone I loved bounce off the ground would have been horrific and what I did see was sickening enough all on its own. It took me another 5 or 6 seconds to get to the ground near to where I had seen her land. From the air I could see everyone running from the drop zone towards the end of the runway as I spiralled down, cut away my main parachute and went to find her.

I was the first person there, seconds before everyone else, terrified of what I was going to see, not wanting to look, but having to, sure she was bound to be dead. I found her lying on her on her back, her face was covered with blood as she spat out teeth and coughed to clear her throat, trying to speak. Her left leg was bent at a strange angle, obviously broken, but she was conscious, aware of where she was and alive. I was astounded, I just couldn't believe it, no one *could have survived this, let alone be awake and trying to speak. Relief just engulfed me, mixed with shock and the need to get help immediately taking over, but I felt rooted to the spot, unable to move, confused and helpless, feeling the blood drain from my face. Suddenly everyone was there, taking over and doing what needed to be done. Afterwards they described the multiple scenarios rushing through their mind of what they thought they would find, a dead body, a paralysed person with no pain, massive injuries that would kill her before the ambulance arrived, or at the very least, unconscious.*

I seemed to be watching the mad flurry of activity and conversations about the best thing to do from afar, not taking part, just standing there. It was a scene of controlled frenzy and those who knew a little of what to do were doing their best to keep Joanne safe and all I could do was hope the ambulance would come quickly. After an initial silence which only seemed to last seconds, Joanne began screaming in pain, and asking us to put her leg down, but it was already flat, at an odd angle. The sound was awful, a kind of scream

I had never heard before and, thankfully, never have again. A friend held her hand reassuring her that everything would be OK, but nobody knew if that was going to be true, we had no idea how seriously injured she was.

After the initial rush there was nothing we could do but wait for help to arrive. There was an eerie silence as we all stood around her, the peace only interrupted by her screaming and the low whispering of our friend keeping her company and listening when she tried to speak. As always, Joanne was trying to take control of the situation, mumbling not to take her helmet off or move her. Even then, although she must have been terrified, she was trying to reassure us that she was ok and telling us the injuries she thought she had, but she couldn't speak properly, her face looked a mess, and she could hardly open her mouth.

The ambulance seemed to take forever, but finally it arrived. One of our friends recalls he was worried as the paramedics seemed to be a bit out of their depth with such a serious accident, although they wouldn't have known what they were going to find either when they arrived. It's hard to imagine that mobile phones were only part of daily life for some and no one at the club had one. The ambulance had been rung on the landline as soon as those on the ground realised what was happening in the sky, they didn't have any details to give to emergency services except, "get here fast!" If the accident had happened now, pictures may have been taken, posts on social media sent and videos recorded to capture all the gory details.

As Joanne was stabilised and the pain relief began to work, we all lifted her out of the clearing to the ambulance. It was only then that I panicked, I had remembered the boys were still at the clubhouse and I had no idea if anyone had told them it was Joanne that had hit the ground and that she was alive. I was hoping above all that they hadn't seen what had happened, as we had left them playing, being looked after by friends who were still with them and who would take them somewhere safe where I could collect them as soon as I knew Joanne would be alright and what her injuries were.

I went in the ambulance, and it seemed I waited a lifetime in the waiting room with our friend Adam, listening to Joanne screaming, cursing, and then apologising. If there was anything that lightened the mood the "sorry", was it. It seemed ages before anyone told us what was going on. The doctor told us what he knew, but she needed more in-depth scans to check for internal damage and they were going to transfer her to the Royal Victoria Hospital in Belfast. With such a serious trauma it was better she went straight there, and she had quite a list of broken bones; her leg, arm, pelvis and multiple fractures of her face, jaw, cheekbones, and lots of broken teeth. Although they had stabilised her and filled her up with pain relief, they couldn't tell me for sure that she was out of the woods just yet.

I went in to see her then and she was still conscious, they had cleaned her up and she was in a haze of morphine but giving off because they had cut off her jumpsuit and favourite clothes. As I kissed her, I explained that I would get the boys and contact her parents, telling her she would be alright, but thinking, "I hope you will be. Please, please just survive".

After a while I dragged myself away to find out where the boys had been taken to and bring them home. I was still in shock, unsure of what they would have been told and working out what I would say to them to reassure them that their mum was alive but had serious injuries. At their age they could accept it as children do, or be terrified, or anything in between. How was I going to tell Joanne's parents, who had never wanted her to jump in the first place and had been proven right that skydiving could go so wrong? Would they blame me for getting her involved in the first place? How could I tell anyone my part in this when they asked? It was then that the events of the jump hit me. How could I have done something so stupid, a momentary decision that ended up like this? I felt sick to the pit of my stomach, with all-consuming guilt and fearful that that would be the last time I would see her alive.

When I got back to the drop zone there was a small, subdued party going on, a "Joanne's alive" party which is *typical of the mindset of the Blueskies jumpers. Everyone was asking over and over what happened, but I couldn't give them all the details, I hadn't processed them myself yet. Maybe I was too scared for myself, knowing there would be an investigation, or I didn't want to lose credibility as an instructor, burst my bubble that I couldn't make mistakes, but whatever the reason, I struggled to tell them about my part in the accident and began to blame Joanne for doing the second turn and just opening far too low. Everyone chose to believe it and I could feel myself begin to be protected by the inner circle of skydivers, all coming together to "have my back" and it was a simple explanation, not one that would raise questions or ever stop any of them jumping again. If they had to choose between who to support, I knew it would be me and that Joanne, as she wasn't so experienced, would become less and less part of the club, especially if she couldn't jump again. I didn't mention that I had come down in front of her and distracted her, I knew I was covering up the real events right from the start. I thought, "I'll tell them when everything has died down", but it would be a year later before I did.*

By then it was nearly midnight, and the boys were asleep, I waited until early morning to bring them home. Alex and Matthew were their usual bubbly selves, but Aaron was quiet and reserved. I didn't know it at the time, but he had seen the accident and overheard the adults taking about it, no one thought to speak to him directly to let him know his mum was ok. I answered their questions and comforted them as best I could as I got them ready to go to their grandparents.

The hardest phone-call I ever had to make was to Joanne's mum and dad to tell them what had happened. As soon as they heard the phone ringing in the middle of the night, they would know something terrible had happened. I told them what I knew at that time, that she had gone to the Royal and I had the boys, but again there were too many questions for my head to compute, I was in a daze, the adrenaline had stopped pumping. It was only when the boys left with their grandfather that I was finally on my own and the enormity of what happened took over and the bottled-up

emotion and trauma flooded out of me."

Chapter Five

A Little Less Broken

Waking up from surgery is completely disorientating. Faces swimming around, *"you're Ok, it's all over"*, *"are you sore?"* The sterile surroundings of machines, wires, drips, oxygen masks and paper gowns. It took a few minutes to take it all in, and for me to remember how I had got there. It was surreal, I had just woken up, was it a dream? The agony had gone, replaced by a much more controlled operation pain and I felt that I had been put together again, that I was a little less "broken".

I scanned my body, hardly daring to look at what surgery had been needed. I could feel all my limbs and wriggle my toes, that was a good sign. My left arm was in plaster, looking very abnormal; with my hand pointing downwards, I thought; *"that's a bit awkward, but at least it's only my left arm, could've been worse. I can't hear, or talk properly, but at least I can write."*

My left leg was straight again, supported by a pillow under the sheet. I peeked under the sheet at my blue paper gown, no long white plaster sticking to my stomach, maybe no internal injuries? I was nearly laughing with relief … how on earth did I get away with so few injuries?

Suddenly I remembered my face, and as my hand flew up to check I panicked, *"is it a mess, am I scarred forever, have they put it back to how it was?"* It was already beginning to swell and as I felt to check if I had stitches on the outside, I realised that my chin was back in its normal place and all the facial injuries were internal. My tongue explored my broken teeth, some in pieces, but a lot missing too, my gums stitched and thankfully, the front teeth still there, 5 at the front in the top gum, and 7 on the bottom. If I could have, I would have smiled, again thinking how lucky I was. The impact had crushed my teeth and several bones in my face. I could only open my mouth a tiny bit as my jaw was broken, and although the surgeons hadn't wired my jaws they were clamped shut. I could relax now and let the drugs take effect.

The nurse was explaining the surgery I had had, but I could hardly hear because of the speed at which I had fallen, my ears had "popped" and I was also in a beautiful haze of morphine, not sure I was still there at all, a list of injuries felt a bit insignificant in comparison. I remember hearing the list in the background, as I floated in and out, as if I was in a dream.

Many people afterwards asked, *"how on earth did you get away with so few injuries, in fact how are you here at all?"* I couldn't believe it either. Maybe it was because I first hit the ground on my left side, and only on my back after bouncing up into the air again, before coming to rest on the stony grass mound, I had rolled up in a ball before I landed and was being thrown around, so the impact was all on my left side, rather than my back.

That's the physical explanation, but I knew there was a lot more to it than body position. I was always meant to survive. I was given a choice to live before I landed, and had gladly taken it so, no matter how badly I was hurt, I was never going to die.

The day after my surgery my abdomen was rigid with pain, a consultation was requested. I had been working with the consultant surgeon who came to see me the day before my accident, in the surgical outpatient's department. He was known as being one of the most demanding and cantankerous consultants in general surgery. It really was like "Carry on Doctor". In he came, whipped off my top sheet, pulled up my nightdress and asked the huddle of terrified student doctors around my bed, *"well, what do you see?"*

As they seemed to shrink and tried to avoid his gaze, in case they were asked to examine me, I was thinking, *"it depends on what they are looking at",* a multicoloured person covered in bruises, a super-human who survived, or just a naked body. I was mortified, totally exposed to at least ten pairs of eyes, waiting for someone to speak. A few had their turn to poke and prod at my stomach, each asking *"where does it hurt?".* Are you kidding me? Really? *"Around the place you have just poked so hard!"*

A few years later I requested my medical notes as I had intended writing this book much sooner, the never-ending "someday" and I was curious to see what had been recorded, and if there was anything else, or any other injuries that I hadn't known, or had forgotten about.

There in black and white was the harsh, objective, reality of a broken body. In addition to my face, arm and leg that were fixed in the first emergency operation, I found out that I had also had a lacerated liver, fracture in my pelvis and at the back of my skull, severe blood loss that needed multiple transfusions to reverse. The records revealed a more serious picture than I had understood at the time. I don't remember being told about the lacerations in my liver or the fracture at the back of my skull, maybe because they didn't need surgical intervention. The whole emphasis seemed to be on making me ready for discharge and not what I would do afterwards. There was no talk of any "home help," a home visit to check if I would be able to move safely around or any offer of equipment. All these may have been put in place no doubt when I became medically fit for discharge, and had the medical staff finished all they could do, so that planning for my return home could start. I know that I didn't give staff the time to put anything in place. I desperately needed to get home and signed myself out of hospital, against medical advice, after 10 days! Looking back now this was a bit crazy and may not have been the most sensible decision, but I was miserable in hospital, thought I would recover better at home at my own pace and had a sheer stubbornness and determination to get on the road to recovery as fast as I could. It shouldn't have been all about me though. I had not given any thought at all to how I would manage at home, or that I would be totally reliant, and dependent, on Joe and it didn't register with me that it was going to be a long road and not a short sprint to get over this.

The medical notes were focused on the treatment of my physical injuries as those were definitely the priority at the time, and the psychological side was rarely mentioned. In those 10 days in hospital I was traumatised, in a total blur of shock, in fact I was feeling every emotion possible, but no one seemed to notice. My thoughts were a jumbled mess, suffocating me, changing quickly from the elation of *"I survived"*, to the awesome Near-Death Experience, to mounting psychological trauma, self-blame, guilt, recrimination, and anger at myself. *Why did I override the obvious signs not to jump that day and not listen to my intuition? Why had I ever skydived at all?*

I forgot all the reasons I had for jumping, the friends the adrenaline rushes, the freedom - it felt meaningless now.

I felt anxious, overwhelmed and inside I was in turmoil, hidden by a veil of heavy pain relief and sedation, so much so that outwardly I appeared calm and settled to those visiting. It wasn't calmness, it was numbness to everything around me, as if people were doing things to me, but I wasn't there, just going through the motions.

Although there were funny incidents and laughter at visiting time, I remember the first week as a time of overwhelming, constant noise inside my head and around me, many questions to answer and wishing I could be left alone to process what had happened. I was confused, I wanted peace, but was terrified to be left alone, knowing physically I wasn't out of the woods yet, scared to close my eyes and re-live the fall and fear of the unknown for the future.

Reading the nursing notes all those years later, staff looking after me seemed to have missed the emotional side of care with sentences like, *"she told me she thought she was going to die,"* followed by standard statements *"no psychological reference or talk about mood",* and *"not unduly anxious at the time of surgery, or in recovery"*. I'm not sure what they would have done if I had fallen to pieces, screamed and cried all the time, thrown any object close to me or cursed at anyone coming into my room because that was what I wanted to do, but I kept it all in as, if I had let go, I wouldn't have been able to stop.

It's a bit of a shocker becoming a patient when you're a nurse and more than a little bit scary, knowing too much and just hoping no one would kill or harm you by making a mistake. At least it was April. It was a standing joke in work that you don't want to go into hospital in February or August when the new junior doctors started on the wards for the first time and the nurses are running the show.

All the staff I met were hard working and dedicated to their patients, but they were also human, overworked on a busy ward with heavily dependent patients, and unfortunately, I knew as a nurse that a lot that could go wrong and was aware of every possible complication related to my injuries.

I watched everything like a hawk, making sure they were doing what they should have been. When my IV fluids ran out too quickly I turned them off, if they weren't checking my respirations after morphine I did them myself and when they didn't do my observations exactly on time or react quickly enough, didn't get the doctor to write a prescription I needed there or then, I was far too unforgiving, chalking it up on my memory board to remember not to forget these things when I got back to work. Luckily for everyone involved, I couldn't speak much and was in a side-ward out of sight, or I would have become the "nuisance" patient to be avoided at all costs.

When I was on duty on wards, all the staff used to dread when a nurse came in as a patient. They always thought they knew everything about everything and watched, not only the care you were giving them, but also care you gave to others. Sometimes it was written in brackets on their notes after their name, or whispered behind a hand at shift-change, *"she or he's a nurse!"* Somehow you could always clear a side-ward to move them into if they were making the staff's life a misery and while they thought they were getting a perk of the job, we had peace and quiet.

Worse still was having a nurse as a patient's next of kin, with no sickness or medication to dull their senses, but we were able to insist on strict visiting times so we could tend to their loved one before the double-doors opened and the onslaught began.

General Nursing can be extremely task orientated and full of routines, but if these were removed there would be chaos and no structure for the day. This makes it hard to allow for the personal touch, the "hand-holding" and emotional support I had thought nursing was all about when I chose it as a career. The endless bureaucracy of paperwork, assessments, recording for assurances that you were giving the care you were meant to and time it took to do this has got longer and longer, taking away from being with the person. The agenda is to make care an individual experience, but this is very difficult to achieve. In fact, if you sat down with the patient to give them some time you knew that was taking away from a task, or putting more work onto colleagues, neither of which you wanted to do, yet to me, as someone who had just come through a major accident and was traumatised, scared and anxious the time nurses spent with me, just to talk or reassure me that I would be OK was vital.

For staff there are definite expectations that a patient will achieve certain things on each day from when a person comes in until they go home. This is my (tongue-in-cheek) roadmap for the perfect patient journey.

Day 1:

OK, you can have the first day to wake up and a button to control your own pain-relief. If you are lucky this goes on for 2 or 3 days.

Day 2 or 3:

The flurry of excitement starts. Drips down, catheter out, nightdress changed, all so you can be out of bed, sitting up, bravely smiling through the realisation that pain is now part of life, for the event of the morning, the ward round. It's a bit like being in the army, with the practice of "hurry up and wait". Don't look too healthy though, or you may never be allowed to get back into bed again.

Day 4:

Walk the length of the corridor and climb a set of stairs. Success. After that, well, your white patient-property bags could be packed, and you could be well on your way out the door. A good job well done.

Well, that's the aim, but my journey took a bit longer.

One of the most obvious "tasks" was getting up in the morning to get washed and dressed, a major starting point on your road back to independence. One thing I remember being drummed into us as we trained was not to forget the patient is there or talk over them if two nurses are working together. I laughed to myself when this happened each day and I knew more about the nurses' private lives than I wanted to and heard all the ward gossip as they made my bed and helped me get washed. I could see why this was happening. I wasn't the most communitive at the time, the witty comments I would normally come out with were eluding me and small talk took too much effort. I listened into their chat about boyfriends, including what they got up to together, their kids and holidays, that brought a normality into the room and took away from the abnormal situation I was in. Would I ever be back to ward life, back to nursing, and be the one helping instead of being helped any time soon, discussing those things with my colleagues, or was everything going to change for me? I just didn't know the answer.

It wasn't possible for the nurses to spend any more time with me than they did so I never felt properly clean, only having "a lick and a promise" as my granny would have said. The old nursing practice of total bed-baths and hair-washings were out and staying in bed for days wasn't an option. The aim was to get you out of bed as quickly as possible so you could do these things yourself. A full bath or shower was out of the question, but it would have been fantastic.

In my notes, by day 5, it was recorded that I was "independent with hygiene," which was a bit of an exaggeration, in fact it was totally fictional. I had never felt more dysfunctional in my life. I remember being left with a basin of water, soap, and a toothbrush every day, because that was what everyone got, and part of the routine. To me it felt thoughtless, I couldn't use the toothbrush as my mouth was stitched up and most of my teeth were missing or have much success with washing as my arm was in plaster. As I looked at these everyday things that I had taken for granted a few days before, wondering what to try first, or whether to bother at all, I realised how tiny my life had become compared to how full, busy, and hectic it had been, total independence to total dependence in a blink of an eye.

There is little privacy in hospital, and I had to leave my pride and dignity at the door. I never thought I'd be using a commode or have someone washing and dressing me. I knew I must have looked a mess, as I was multi coloured with bruising, and swollen from top to toe, and the glamour of make-up and hair done properly was totally unimportant, whereas beforehand I wouldn't have gone out without it. No-one had given me a mirror when I was lying in bed, I hadn't wanted one, but it came as part of the basin and soap package, so I had to pluck up the courage to look. It was the strangest feeling when I saw my face for the first time and for a split second, I didn't recognise myself. My face looked shorter and was a swollen, bruised mess. I couldn't make out my features or imagine how I would look when the swelling went down. *Would I still be loved looking like this? Would the boys recognise me, or be terrified at the way I looked? Would I ever be able to smile again?* I felt like my identity had gone. I felt like I was a stranger to myself.

Other memories of the first few days in hospital are a bit of a blur and have faded over the years, but I still remember pints of blood and the pain relief pump that was taken away too soon. After a couple of days on this amount of pain relief you get a false sense of security about the level of pain you will have without it. The morphine was replaced by tablets at regular times instead and its agony when the morphine wears off and the actual pain kicks in. Getting out of, and sitting beside the bed was a major milestone, but it felt like I was sitting on glass. When I was in the chair I couldn't get back into bed on my own and on the first day my buzzer for attention was at the top of my bed, too far for me to reach and I had to wait until someone came into my room to rescue me. It was the same with the commode, praying my visitors wouldn't come in while I was on it, or that it would still be in the room when they arrived. And then came moving and walking again. The only way I could describe physiotherapists were "those who inflict pain" and I christened my very own "the bitch from hell." If I could have, I would have hidden somewhere, but I was a captive in my room, and of course a fast getaway was out of the question, I couldn't avoid her. I'm sure she was a good person, but I swear I could see horns and a forked tail poking out of her tunic. The therapists came in the morning, like a flock of hungry seagulls on a mission in their white uniforms, fanning out into every part of the ward with strange pieces of equipment that you knew would be a new form of torture. My physiotherapist, aka the bitch from hell, was determined to get me walking, or in my case hopping, as soon as possible and I understood that staying in bed was a recipe for blood-clots and chest infections, but it was hard, painful, and slow. It was then that the penny dropped, and I came face to face with the reality of the serious injuries I had and the effort it would take to heal physically. This was both daunting and scary as I imagined the road to recovery stretching out in front of me, never knowing when it would end. As my left arm was in plaster and I wasn't to put any weight on my left leg I had to use a pulpit frame. This surrounds you so that you can rest your arms on it while holding the handles. I can still picture the length of the ward from my room to the double entrance doors, drip attached to the frame and the physio walking along beside me with a bowl in case I was sick. My low blood count made me nauseous and dizzy, but she was going to make me walk the full length of the ward and back if it killed her, or me. But then, when I had got comfortably back into bed, she arrived with an even more horrendous torture tool, "The Passive Exerciser". This moved my broken leg back and forward, but if I was left alone, I couldn't get off it or find the off button, and I was terrified it would speed up, I was completely at her mercy, especially if she went on her tea-break. I toyed with the idea of using reverse psychology and telling her it was my favourite exercise, hopeful that she might think I liked it too much and take it off me, but the risk of further punishment was too great. I resigned myself to letting her do whatever she wanted to me and get on with it, as I hoped it was all for the greater good.

Each day I had to work on getting my mouth to open. To begin with I could only get the tip of a spoon or a straw in and then tongue depressors like lolly-pop sticks were built up one by one each day until finally, after a few weeks, I could open my mouth wide enough to begin to eat and talk properly again. I could only eat pureed food, when the tray came in and the metal lid was lifted the plate usually had a brown dollop of meat or mince, a white mound of potato, and whatever colour the vegetables were on that day. It had no bulk and I felt hungry all the time and if I ever see a Petit Filous yogurt or jelly again, it will be too soon! At one meal I was making my way through pureed turnip when I felt a sharp object in my mouth. To my horror it was a sliver of glass, it had cut my stitches and my mouth was bleeding. All I could think of were the old people on the ward on the same diet as me. By the time I had got up and out of my room in my frame the dinners were over, all I could do was report it and hope that no one else had eaten it. It was also frustrating when my meal was left on the table at the end of the bed. I couldn't reach it. The nursing assistant would come in, lift the lid, and declare, *"you're not hungry then?"* and whip it out of the room before I had the chance to tell her I was starving. As time went by, when I got home, I found my favourite meals to puree. Chinese gravy, chips and mushrooms or chicken dinners are delicious when they're blended.

My mother brought the boys into visit after a few days. I remember them standing at the door looking in, three red-headed steppingstones, one above the other and I was ecstatic to see them. The last time had been during the near-death experience, before I hit the ground, when I chose to come back to them. They must have been warned not to come near me or touch me and I'm sure they were shocked, maybe scared at what they saw and probably worried that they would hurt me, but all I wanted was to hold them and tell them I was going to be okay, we were all going to be okay and that I'd be home soon. This mummy in the bed was so different from the mummy they had last seen, and I wasn't able to get up and walk over to them or even give them a decent hug to reassure them.

The only glimpse I got of their experience was when Aaron had to write a story about an event he remembered. Aaron was 10 years old by that time, one year later, but it was so descriptive, right down to the smell of the hospital, the way I looked and what he had felt like. I still feel like crying with overwhelming guilt when I remember it. His teacher, after she had read it, contacted me to congratulate me on how imaginative he was, but I quickly filled her in that it was all true.

At that stage no matter how much shock I was in, I felt the beginning of hope and resolution to push myself to become as strong and fit as I was before, or even better than that. It was time to appreciate how amazing the body is at healing and protecting so I just had to wait to see how well mine could do this. Joe and my children were my reason to push forward and keep going. I had had some major difficulties and problems to solve by that time in my life and had got through them, I knew I could do it again, even though I felt like I was starting from scratch.

That first week in hospital I had quite a few visitors, fellow jumpers, and family. People would also come to the door and look in and walk away without saying anything which was such a strange thing to do. I worked in the Royal so of course I was the talk of the place that week and it was surreal seeing my accident reported on the main evening news and in the paper. I had refused to give an interview or have my picture taken and Joe wasn't asked to contribute to any articles that were printed so they were mostly inaccurate. The chief skydiving instructor was interviewed at Bishopscourt the next day, he hadn't been there on the day of the accident and couldn't have known the full story. His interview with the local news channel only made me angry as I was held totally to blame and painted as a "blonde bimbo" who had messed up. For years I felt I had missed out on giving my version of events right from the start, but the first week wasn't the time to go into depth about what had happened. Joe and I hadn't had the chance to speak properly about the jump and the events that unfolded, we were in shock, and we couldn't take in the enormity of what we had experienced.

The week wasn't all struggle, there were many funny times as well. The banter and dark humour from my visitors kept me going, breaking up the day, rescuing me from my own thoughts. I could tell people were nervous around me, but also in amazement that I was alive. My work mates came to wash my hair and give me a proper clean and as embarrassing as it was, it was heaven. It's those little things that matter so much.

The first weekend after the accident arrived and the visitors stopped coming. Our skydiving friends were down at the club, my family had came and went and all that was left was the mundane routine of the hospital. I don't think I can remember a time when I had felt lonely, abandoned, and scared. I didn't want to be on my own with too much time to think, too much time to recall the enormity of the accident. The stark reality hit, that my life had turned upside down, stopped dead in its tracks, but everyone else's went straight back to normal. Joe had gone to the club too, to "get back on the saddle", see how he would feel and all I could think was, *"what a selfish git! How could you do this to me so soon? Is this what it'll be like, I lie at home, injured by the very sport that you still get to enjoy?"* I knew he'd be in the middle of it all, impressing the students, laughing, joking with our friends, kitting up, jumping, and forgetting about me.

This couldn't have been further from the truth; we were beginning to react differently to the horrific trauma we had been through. I was full of self-pity, insecurity, and fear while he was testing himself, finding out if he could jump again, needing the familiar when everything had changed and our friends and an escape for a day from seeing the results of the accident, he felt he had caused.

I knew then that I would never jump again, even if I wanted to. The pressure that would be put on me from others would be too great and no one, except those in the sport, would understand why I would put myself in that situation again. I felt like it was one of the main things I had chosen to do in my life at that time and now it was taken away by other's expectations. But I suppose that if I had to leave jumping behind it was better to leave in style … and you don't get much more memorable than the way I did it. I had succeeded in my 360-degree turn, it had been the ultimate skydive so I would never be able to top it for an unbelievable experience, thrill, and survival.

As my drips came down and I could get in and out of bed, more or less independently, I automatically wanted to go home. I craved my own space with all my familiar things around me so that I could check that everything I knew hadn't been taken away from me, that normality still existed. I wanted my own bed, to sleep for hours, to be kissed and hugged in private, lie with my head on Joe's shoulder and become the girlfriend and mother again, not the patient.

The Easter holidays were over, and the boys had to go back to school. My parents did offer to take me to their house and help with the boys, but I needed Joe and his love, support and understanding and there was no way I was going to cause any more upheaval to the boys than I had to. They had also got the shock of their lives and needed things to go back to normal. I didn't question how this would work or how I would manage, I don't remember if Joe and I even had a serious talk about what we needed to do or asked for any help for when we got home. On the Tuesday I told the doctors I was going. They were a bit shocked, tried to talk me out of it and advised against it, but I was adamant, and after giving me a few more pints of blood and making their preparations for my discharge, I signed myself out. I sat there, ready and waiting for Joe to pick me up, still in my pyjamas as my clothes were too difficult to get into, surrounded by hospital bags stuffed with my belongings, "get-well soon" cards and treats I couldn't eat, feeling an excited and fearful anticipation for what lay ahead.

Act Three

The Aftermath

"… I'll wipe away those bitter tears

I'll chase away those restless fears

That turn your blue skies into grey

Why Worry? There should be laughter after pain …"

- **Why Worry? – Dire Straits**

Chapter Six

Back to Life, Back to

Reality

Imagine if you put the onslaught of the healing of my physical injuries, the psychological effects of trauma and the enormity of the insight I gained from my near-death experience into a blender and blitzed them, the mix would contain all the positive and negative ingredients that helped and hindered my road to recovery.

Following the accident, the psychological effects of a traumatic event, coupled with those of a near-death experience, were so entwined that it is impossible to now unpick them and attribute them to any one element. Several manifest themselves in the same way and resulted in the need to adapt in many ways; difficulties communicating and engaging with others, mood swings, changes in belief systems and values, fear and uncertainty and loss of control in areas of life that were taken for granted before. It's also impossible to completely label or categorise these feelings as many will be expected, such as frustration from immobility, or come from personality traits I already had and my background or upbringing. To me there is always a danger in a diagnosis and the confusion of trying to piece it all together is mind-blowing.

I know I brought many of those emotions and feelings with me into the accident; the insecurities, fear of abandonment, lack of confidence and low self-worth, they weren't new, but after the accident they were at a whole new level.

The broken bones and other injuries took an expected route to healing, albeit after several surgeries, long-term dental work carried on in the background, and the ongoing pain just exacerbated the symptoms of trauma. They served to remind me of the accident every day and undermined my self-image and confidence every time I smiled. The positive side of me was also there, it hadn't left. The love for my nearest and dearest, the resilience, strength of character, determination, half-full approach, and humour still bubbled up to the surface.

Until I could walk again unaided, after a year and a half, the physical injuries were a major obstacle to overcome. The first taster of how much physical healing I needed came the minute I said goodbye and the doors of the ward closed behind me. Anyone who has come home from hospital will know what a shock to the system it is. You think you are so capable, but on the ward you are only walking from the bed to the chair or down a corridor, not having to navigate hazards and with a seat or wheelchair there to catch you if you couldn't go any further. Any criticisms of the care I received, which were few, paled into insignificance when I realised the enormity of the task others would have to do for me just to manage day to day.

I really should have listened to everyone when they told me not to go home early and I wished I had gone straight back to the ward. As soon as I made it to the front door, I had reached the point of no return and someone else would soon be in my still-warm bed. It was hard just getting to the car in the carpark, I insisted on walking when Joe could have driven to the door, this was lesson one in how my obstinacy did not match my physical ability and there would be many more lessons like this to be learned.

Every curb was an obstacle and the uneven surfaces, or slopes on the pavements were danger zones, never noticed before, but now I was watching every step, convinced I was going to tip over and fall. I became conscious of passer-by's looking curiously at my bruised swollen face and at me hopping down the road on crutches.

They were also sizing Joe up, maybe imagining he had done this to me, or that I was making a run for it, as I was still in my pyjamas. If we had had mobile phones and social media, I'm sure my attempts to get in and out of the car would have "gone viral", in hindsight hilarious, but at the time painful and frustrating, and *"how do you get 10 elephants into a mini?"* comes to mind. In the end we had to put the backseat down and I slid into the car through the boot to lie down, vowing to practice again later, or avoid going out ever again.

I had forgotten, or never noticed, how inaccessible my house was. There were steps everywhere – up to the front door, into the house and out to the back. I hadn't remembered that the banister on the stairs didn't go the whole way up, and it wouldn't be possible to climb them for a few weeks. When I finally did, to sleep in my own bed, use a toilet instead of a bucket and get a bath, was heaven, but it took months for the images of ground rush and absolute fear of falling to stop when I went to the top of the stairs to go down again.

Joe and I were in total shock when we finally sat down, exhausted, after the marathon effort to get home and into the house for the first time. *How did we leave the house on a perfectly normal and beautiful Spring Day and come home to our lives completely changed?* As we silently looked at each other, not knowing what to say or do, alone for the first time, I knew we were both thinking, *"what the frig happened there, was that a total nightmare, or did it really happen?"* One of those "before and after" events that would stick with us and change us for the rest of our lives, we just didn't know how, or to what extent, at the time.

In those first few months of enforced rest, I had time to give concentrated love and attention to the children and this was needed for them, and for me. At times I must have smothered them, wanting to hold them all the time and terrified that something would happen to them if they left the house. My priorities had been to be the provider, to give them the basics and, like most working people, I had to juggle the long hours on shift work, studying and the additional care Matthew needed. I was stopped in my tracks, that side of my life gone for a while and if you can be grateful for bedrest after an accident, this is the reason. On many occasions, they would jump in beside me on the pull-out bed I slept on downstairs, to watch their favourite videos for hours, toys were everywhere, spilt cereal and juice on the floor, noise, laughs and tantrums, life lived in the one room. Of course, there was also the never-ending game of "hide mummy's crutches" or sneaking treats from the kitchen when I couldn't stop them.

In a perfect world, I would get as much care I needed, provided by the NHS at a time I wanted it, and at home. This would be totally unrealistic today, and was then, as there was little help for anyone younger than 65 years. The help and support I got from others could never have matched my needs; physically or mentally and for as long as I needed it, as it was 24 hours a day, 7 days per week. The only place I would have got that was in hospital and I had decided to leave too early, without thinking of how I would manage, or the pressure I would put on Joe and others to look after me.

In our family we had never had to care for anyone long-term or do some of the intimate and practical tasks involved, this situation was new to everyone and, to be fair, neither Joe nor I told anyone how hard it was or the details of everything I needed. We had a standing joke in our family that you were allowed to have sympathy and stay in bed for three days, no matter what was wrong. and after that there was no need to "wallow in self-pity, get up and get on with it". I came from hardy, and stubborn stock, but this helped me to persevere when I needed all the strength I could muster.

I found the most frustrating part of dependence is that you lose control over so many aspects of life, normal choices like what clothes to wear, when to get washed and dressed, and watch someone else do household tasks, while biting your tongue when it wasn't the way you would have done it. My care and psychological support had to revolve around everyone else's plans, especially family and friends who wanted to help, but had limited time. I had to content myself with "fitting in", and this wasn't always when I wanted or needed help, but I knew if I didn't accept it then I'd miss the time they did have to spare. I didn't know what was worse, feeling selfish that this thought would enter my head at all, ungrateful if they did want to help and I didn't accept it, feeling like the ultimate burden, or speaking up and saying, *"I'm too sore"* or *"I just want to be alone at the minute, but please come back".* That is the reality of the situation, other people must go back to their normal lives regardless, it was hard to watch though.

Joe was amazing, though he has told me since he was terrified when I came out of hospital early, as he didn't have a clue what to do. Suddenly, he had to take on the role of carer and I relied on him totally. I already knew he was loving and caring, and this shone through every day, helping me get washed, dressed, and get to the toilet …well holding me as I hovered over a bucket when I couldn't get upstairs, pureeing my food for the day before he went to work and, of course, doing everything for the boys. Natalie was there too to help and stayed with us most of the time, I was rarely on my own. I will be forever grateful for the help I got so I could get back on my feet, from friends calling in and my mum and dad keeping the boys at the weekend as often as they could to my brother and sister ringing from Scotland to see how I was.

I often think to myself that if the same accident happened now, I wouldn't recover so well. Of course, physically I'm older and I wouldn't heal as quickly, but I would be so spoiled by Joe and my children, that I would have too much care. *This sounds ridiculous, but if there is no need to do anything why would you push yourself as hard?* To do things for yourself and be independent is a vital part of recovery, it is then your accomplishment, with the pride that comes from reaching even the smallest of goals, is a way back to some kind of normality, whatever that looks like.

After six weeks I got the plaster off my arm, a first tangible sign that I was healing, and another tiny step towards independence, but my leg didn't heal straight away. I broke the holding screws that stabilised the pin in my leg, and the fracture was not healing as it should have done. I had two more operations, but it wasn't until I had bone grafting a year later that my leg fracture finally united and I could begin to walk independently. Each time I had an operation I felt I had to start again from scratch; on crutches, more pain, bedrest, and dependency, but unlike the first emergency operation, in those first few hours after the accident, these were planned, I knew what to expect, each time it became easier, and I knew I would manage.

I remember my last out-patients appointment about 18 months after the accident. I had walked in without my crutches, thinking I was great, looking forward to the X-ray that would confirm I had finally been put back together again. I was still limping heavily, but the consultant said to me, *"why are you still limping, we've fixed you"*. I recalled his words every time I walked, until a few weeks later I stopped limping. It was such a real sense of achievement. I hoped, but never thought, I would walk properly again. Gritty determination and a goal never to give up had kept me going until I got to that stage.

By far though, my facial injuries and loss of teeth took the longest to heal and needed the most work. I met the dentist a couple of months after the accident, and I'm sure neither of us imagined that it would take 15 years of treatment for me to smile without being self-conscious. He tried to save as many teeth as possible and put in bridges, but he couldn't do much work to begin with as I still couldn't open my mouth wide and there were many times the NHS wouldn't pay for the tooth salvage I needed as removing them was cheaper and I could survive with just front teeth. I suppose fixing my teeth was a learning curve for him too. I had lost a lot of gum and my mouth couldn't hold dentures but eventually I got my tooth implants, I could smile with confidence again and had new cheekbones made from artificial bone, there's always a silver lining.

I also wanted to prove I could be better, stronger, thinner, than before. I wanted to show people I was not going to be outwardly physically disabled, and whilst keeping my trauma secret, I would look like I had fully recovered. I often turned my back on the advice from others, especially programmes set up by community teams for physical rehabilitation, not through obstinacy or unwillingness, but because I needed to adjust to the physical pace I was at and could tolerate. Their goals weren't realistic to me, sometimes not quick enough and sometimes too hard. I knew I was determined enough to achieve what I needed to in the long-term and could work out a plan for myself. In that first year after the accident, I found out how much I loved the gym, something I hadn't done before, and I went even with a broken left leg to strengthen the upper half of my body and my other leg. I used to get some stares cycling with only one leg and the crutches to the side. As time went on and I became physically strong again, the gym became an obsession for several years and I wouldn't eat if I wasn't going to the gym the next day. I pushed myself so hard when I was there and wouldn't leave until I had burned at least 2,000 calories.

Not surprisingly I became very thin, but I still didn't feel as strong or beautiful as I thought I would. It was like changing one adrenaline rush for another and I came to love the endorphins from hard exercise. I knew that I was replacing an addiction to skydiving and the feelings it gave me, with another, that could never match the intensity of the aftermath of a jump but that gave me something to focus on and progress that I could see, no matter how hard it was or what pain I was in.

The Verve got it right when they sang, *"the drugs don't work, they just make it worse…"*, as by far the most difficult aspect of recovery was controlling my pain, and then, when I did, overcoming a dependence on painkillers I had developed as a result. In the beginning I had that compulsive craving to over-take whatever I was prescribed, no amount was enough to dull the on-going physical pain, firstly so that I could regain my independence and look after the children, but more often to escape the emotional pain of the persistent memories of the trauma. I needed to level my unpredictable emotions, which seemed to be all over the place, to remain calm and get through every day. In a strange way, they gave me a sense of control, but the feelings are false, the warm codeine hugs and feelings of happiness and calm are only a mask, dulling your motivation to heal or deal with the difficulties you are having without the drugs. Ultimately, they zap your self-esteem and mental health. Something else to conquer and overcome and this can feel like too much of a mountain to climb.

I had never had strong pain relief before, even when having my children. I had my first syringe of morphine when I was in agony at the accident site, and I got hooked. As time went on and I left hospital I still needed medication for physical pain, but very soon I knew the cocktails of drugs I was given would ease both the physical and mental pain, neither of which would go away. Pain relief came on repeat prescription and because my leg didn't heal properly it was assumed that I must be in agony, and most of the time I was, so I was given higher and higher doses until I had a locked cupboard in the house full of any amount and type of medication I could possibly want. I can still see it in my mind's eye, opening the cupboard to choose what to take depending on my level of pain, the mood I was in, or what I had to get done in the day; as casually done as looking for ingredients to make dinner, but much more satisfying.

It was after the last operation and when my leg had healed that I went to my G.P. to talk about my medication. It was the scariest and bravest thing I had to do. I couldn't possibly carry on in a haze of medication and I knew deep down that I didn't need as much to dampen the physical pain, but I was terrified that I wouldn't cope without them psychologically. My dream of getting back to nursing would be over, not because of my physical injuries, but because of addiction. It would be impossible to do a medicine round with a trolley full of drugs without the temptation of taking some myself, risking my nursing registration, causing harm to patients and all the fall-out of that. Even so, I was in two minds before I went to confess. *Would it be bad to give up nursing so I could keep the drugs? Could I get away with it, no one would notice? What's so bad about using it to blunt the memories?* That's what the psychological mess of dependence leaves you with.

I had a great G.P. who was ready to help and saw me through that first year with care and empathy. I began the battle to reduce the strength of the medications I was on first, and as I reduced them, I found I could get used to some level of pain, but I wanted none, which was totally unrealistic. I feared pain, and still do today, mine was relentless and, on many occasions, I let it bring me down, depress me and make me feel older than my years, but over recent years I have resigned myself to the fact that the nagging, toothache-like pain in my bones is here to stay. Sometimes I wake up feeling like I have been hit by a bus, but I have come to realise that if that's the worst outcome from the accident then that's OK. It reminds me I am still alive and kicking. Physical or psychological hurt, pain is pain and of course medication can help, but it is no longer the crutch I used as the panacea for all my troubles, it's just another challenge I had to overcome.

It's amazing how a body can heal and I'm in awe when I remember how it crumpled when I hit the ground, to be fixed to the extent that now no one would know that I had

had the accident at all. All the scars are hidden, and I don't even notice them anymore, they are a reminder of recovery, a life event. The immediate shock to my physical body began to fade over the next year and with each new milestone achieved I began having hope that, even though my life would be different, I survived, and I was able to function. I began to feel that I would get back to independence at some stage and it wouldn't be like this forever. My thought patterns were changing from *"I'll never be able to do this"* to a tentative, *"I think I will be ok"*.

Chapter Seven

The Trauma of Trauma

Trauma is all around us, horrific traumas, portrayed on the news, social media, a barrage of information on famines, volcano eruptions that eradicate whole villages leaving nothing behind, car accidents, shootings, bombings. Indiscriminate adversity is part of being human and is an intertwined and inevitable part of being alive.

There is no hierarchy in trauma, what is trauma to one person will not be to another, and it doesn't need to come from a major accident or an event that hits the news, to feel its effects. It is only when trauma happens to you, or those you know, that this ongoing background noise becomes real. In the blink of an eye, everything can change, and not only do you have to change directions, but you also have a new identity. For me this was not only physical, but emotional and psychological as well, and affected all areas of my life from being dependent due to my injuries, facial injuries testing my sense of identity to trauma symptoms of mental health difficulties, addiction to pain relief, and navigating relationships, while always fighting to regain control of my life. Immediately after the accident I assumed I would be so traumatised I wouldn't remember anything straight away, but that took months and years, and a lot of practice to squash it into that hidden suitcase so I could zip it up and forget about it.

Remembering it now, it was a period in my life of utter confusion. I had not been that moody, angry, and frustrated person before the accident and most of the time I didn't recognise myself. I could feel my behaviour and communication changing, from day-to-day conversations to major choices. I couldn't cope with problems in the same way, was over-reacting to the simplest of things, or comments which would never have bothered me before. I hated that my usual kind, soft way of approaching things was now filled with resentment, jealousy, and mood swings. I had no idea what was going on, there was no one to advise me and no information to find out for myself at that time, when there was a lack of specialist help and I had no internet or computer to search for answers. I wish I had known that after such an event I would have an indelible footprint and vivid picture of trauma in my brain, one I know I still have despite the length of time that has gone by, faded but still there. I may not have been so hard on myself in the beginning and understood that I wasn't going mad but having normal reactions to a horrible experience and I would have had hope in the knowledge that the acute, immediate reactions would dull in time and the positive would shine out again. Although the effects I describe seem negatively all-consuming, they were only part of my life, but they dominated my thought processes for the first few years, I was still able to move forward in my home and work life, achieving more than I expected through determination, the knowledge that I wanted to live life to the full and be the best mother and partner I could be. However, a dulled form of trauma sat inside me as a background pressure I felt all the time in my chest. A heaviness, that became familiar, but I couldn't put my finger on what it was. I only realised what this had been when it left me, in that clearing on my visit back to the accident site, and I accepted that the accident had really happened and wasn't a dream, or a story I read.

My brain was having a tug of war between negativity and positivity, and I felt that an endless set of problems and bad memories were swirling around in my head, making me crazy. I was having multiple flashbacks in the first year, seeing snippets of the accident and the ground rushing up to grab me, unpredictable and, like a black-out, I was totally unaware of the world around me during them. It was like my brain was trying to relive the whole thing on a presentation loop, trying to find somewhere to store the details.

I remember collecting the boys from school one day and I was on crutches, trying to keep up with them as they ran ahead, going as fast as I could. Suddenly it happened again, a wave of terror, a feeling of falling and the panic of no control. Everything else faded away, just for a moment, but that was enough to terrify me. What if the boys had run into the road? Was this something else I had to stop doing when I had worked hard to get to the stage where I was strong enough to collect them?

It also happened in the car when I was a passenger and we speeded up or overtook another car. Swirling grass would hit the windscreen, so that all I could see was green, even if I closed my eyes, and I would be clutching onto the dashboard, not letting go until it passed. I thought I was completely losing my mind, but to me these flashbacks also re-enforced that the experience had been real and in a bizarre way this was comforting, I wasn't losing my mind for no reason.

When I was in hospital everyone on that ward had suffered trauma of some kind, and many of the events that led them there would be life changing, like the elderly lady with the fractured hip, who had been lying on the floor for hours waiting for someone to find her, not knowing if she would ever be able to walk properly again or be able to live on her own, or the young man in a car crash, out with his friends, with life-changing injuries and the others injured too. I often wonder what happened to those patients and how they recovered, or were they still scarred by their experience.

Their situations would have been unique and responses individual, but as in my case, the emotional trauma would be too raw to talk about in the early days, but I'm sure knowing the possible effects of trauma would have helped so much when I went home.

I wasn't sleeping properly at all. Every time I closed my eyes and began to drift off, I felt like I was falling, that stage before sleep when you jolt awake before you hit the ground; but I was hitting the ground again and again in a recurring nightmare. If I woke in the middle of the night, when all negative thoughts and worries are always magnified anyway, I was still locked in the memories. Conscious or unconscious I relived it.

I battled to focus on the NDE to bring those positive memories to the fore and replace terror with calm, peace, and the picture of the beautiful place I had been in, and after a while I mastered this, with the nightmares and flashbacks receding over the first year and the positive memories became my "go to" place.

My emotions were all over the place, and usually these were directed at myself more than others. When I read my diary from that time it is coming from a place I don't recognise, the anger, guilt, shame, and self-blame spitting out from the pages.

I was angry for putting myself at risk and that I was now going to have to live with the repercussions and angry at Joe for his part in the accident and then still going to jump. I wanted to be part of the crowd again, telling the stories of the day's jumps, but now I felt abandoned and isolated, lonely in the crowd, regardless of how my friends tried to include me. At the beginning, when I was housebound, our close friends came to us so that I didn't have to go out. Even though I was glad to see them I always felt on the periphery, looking in at the group, hearing myself talking naturally, laughing at jokes, pretending I was having a good time, but on the inside unable to bear the crowd, the noise tiring me out, wanting them to only stay for an hour or two and then leave so it would be quiet again and Joe and I would be on our own. It would have been easy to lose friends, family and let other relationships go, to withdraw into splendid isolation. I wanted those close to me to understand what I was going through without having to tell them, as words to describe it were hard to find to begin with, and it was difficult to have conversations that went deeper than the superficial.

Many times, over the years I have felt a deep, deep sadness, sometimes going on for days or weeks, ending in bouts of depression that were hard to control. To begin with it was outbursts of crying, especially when I was on my own, maybe out of self-pity that the accident had happened to me and feelings that I had lost my former life, grieving for the way it had been before. I was afraid, as if there was an underlying threat at every turn, my world was now riddled with insecurity, safety in the present and future was no longer guaranteed. Thinking about it now, I believe this was when I first realised, how dangerous, brutal, and unpredictable the world and life could be and my naive bubble that bad things only happened to bad people well and truly burst. I found I was much more conscious of trauma, sadness, and fear in other people, so much so, I would suck in these emotions and internalise them, my empathy levels and understanding of what they may be experiencing soaring. The background noise of worldwide and individual's traumas that I wouldn't have given a second thought to before, became all-absorbing and I felt for each and everyone involved, despite not knowing them at all. This was continually exhausting and a heavy burden to carry around.

When I was physically fit, about a year and a half after the accident, I thought I was automatically ready to return to work, I could stand for hours and rush around a busy ward, which was amazing in itself, but I hadn't thought of the psychological strain it would put me under, and over the next ten years I thought I was constantly gathering up traumas in layers on top of my own, or maybe even seeking this out in the choices I made, until front-line work was left behind and I moved into management.

There is no event as traumatic to me, or that has affected me as badly, as the atrocity of the Omagh Bombing on 15th August 1998, three years after my accident.

Anyone my age who grew up in Northern Ireland would have lived through "The Troubles", a period of conflict from 1969 to the signing of The Good Friday

Agreement in 1998 and beyond. The whole community was affected, either directly or indirectly with a continual life of bombs, shootings, intimidation, and political conflict. I began my nurse training in 1989 in Belfast and the physical trauma of gun-shot wounds, murders, beatings, and human suffering because of bombings became "normal" in my nursing practice. This was the final decade of "The Troubles" and there were glimmers of hope, with rumours of peace-talks and paramilitary ceasefires in 1994, 1997 and 1998. However, despite this, in that decade there were 530 deaths, and 10,811 individuals were injured.

It was a Saturday evening; the ward was quiet as several patients had gone home and only the patients who had had the most serious surgeries remained on the monitors. I was working with two other staff until the night duty nurses came in, on a "nightingale" ward, eight beds on each side, no privacy for the patients, but easy for me to see them all at one time. At around five or six in the evening, news began to filter through that a bomb had gone off on a main street in Omagh when unsuspecting people were out doing their normal Saturday shopping, just as you or I would. I only paused for a minute to listen as the patients began to ask for a television to be set up so they could watch the news.

Then the phone began to ring off the hook. Some of the most seriously injured casualties were to be helicoptered to our hospital and my ward was to be cleared as an assessment ward until emergency surgery could be organised. We were joined quickly by senior nurses, doctors and other clinicians and getting equipment ready, moving anyone we could to other wards, or home, and I remember running to the pharmacy for bandages, bags of fluid, and vials of morphine and shoving the overflowing trolley into a side-ward as there was no room in the cupboards. My heart was pounding, we were all anxious and no-one knew quite what to expect as there had been little information passed to us beforehand, we were waiting for the double doors to open and see the first casualty who was wheeled in.

I don't know what I was expecting, but it wasn't the extent of the injuries I saw when the patients arrived.

Despite what I had seen before, I took in the sights of massive injury, sounds of pain and fear and the smells of charred human flesh, blood, and a mixture of metal and engine fumes instead of the clinical, clean, disinfection I was familiar with and went straight back to the first few hours after my accident; fear, panic and the shock of trauma, finding it difficult to hold it in as I went into automatic mode. This was the first time at work that I felt I had totally disengaged from the whole scene around me, trying to save myself and crawl into my NDE place of calm and tranquillity. I was watching the scene unfold as if I was standing apart, not doing anything to help, but of course I was there, in the thick of it, picking shrapnel and glass from skin that felt like sandpaper, comforting a young girl with such bad injuries to her legs we had put up a sheet so she couldn't see them, deflecting her questions, *"will I lose my legs, I can't feel them?", "am I going to survive?",* glad that she had had so much pain relief that she wouldn't remember afterwards. Inwardly crying for how much their lives would change and the recovery journey they were now on, I understood and felt such deep empathy, mixed with anger at the senselessness of it all and sadness that it had happened to them, unlucky to be in the wrong place at the wrong time.

None of us could leave the ward that night and worked on until the casualties left the ward for surgery, all stunned by what we had seen yet accepting it as part of the job, but I knew it had opened a healing scar for me and I was again transported back in time to the rawness of those first few months after the accident. I remembered how much I had wanted to be the nurse then, and not the patient when I was in the same situation, but after this experience I saw the ripples of impact on others involved in any traumatic event, from those caring for you, to family, friends, the wider community, and people completely unknown to the person going through it. After all the effort and determination to get back to nursing, hoping this would be the best place to use my experience to help others, I began to realise that this would only be the case if I ignored the personal cost to my mental health, and I began to think that front-line nursing would not be the best career choice in the long-term.

The following year circumstances at home changed, we needed a bigger house and money was tight; when an opportunity came up to go into prison nursing I took it, not having a clue what it would be like. This wasn't layering up trauma, it was building a wall with Breezeblocks, with trauma everywhere. It's like nowhere else on earth, a concrete jungle, a world within a world, ignored by "outsiders" who wouldn't care what went on inside the walls as long as no one got out. Every part of me was challenged, my belief system, my values and it was a huge shock to the system. I was a fish out of water, and I can't think what possessed me to go there in the first place, except for the great wage. I couldn't get used to the fact that crimes that had traumatised others, or worse, were caused by people who were living "normal" lives, albeit without the freedom we enjoy. All the life-changing insight and learning I had gained from my near-death experience left me during those years, the wonderful feelings, and sensations so totally out of place, with no relevance to the situation I was in. I couldn't understand why others who were working there didn't feel the same way as I did. *Why did I have to feel things so much more intensely? Did no one realise they were wasting the one life they had and had ruined others?* It may appear strange, but I also felt for those who had committed the most serious crimes and the pictures they wouldn't be able to erase from their mind, regardless that they had caused them.

The job overtook my life, the verbal and physical aggression, the manipulation and underlying ongoing threat, the difference in the emergencies we coped with. I worked there for five years, my personality changed for the worse, I drank and partied more and fell into the worst depression I have ever had. The final straw was having to move several times after a security threat with all the upheaval that brought to the family and a totally unexpected epileptic seizure resulting in medical retirement, and no job.

I couldn't believe that 8 years later I was still stuck in a never-ending cycle of negative events without a break, and I began the slippery slope of thinking that my family would be better off without me, that I was a burden and had impacted negatively on everyone around me and I seemed to be the only person in the family to be bringing so much drama to their lives. It had got to the point that when I phoned my family they would always ask, *"what's happened now?"* Something usually had, but I just wanted an "ordinary life". At that point I desperately wanted to go back to the extraordinary place I had been in and take the other path, it would be easier than having to continually move forward and fix my life. How grateful I am that I reached out and asked for help, I can't believe now how I ever thought this, the idea of not being here for my family and having the great life I have now is too awful to contemplate. Again, it was Joe and the kids who were my saving factor. I had had Ella by then and had much to live for, yet it wasn't until I was treated for depression and was able to pick myself up again, I realised that I had been more than able to survive hard times before and would find a way out of this too.

A new job came along, managing a community team back in the NHS and implementing a major project for older people. The next 10 years were the happiest and most fulfilling of my career. I had left many of the trauma triggers behind, my mental and emotional health improved; intrusive, negative thoughts of the accident faded, and life settled down. It was an important lesson to learn and accept that the triggers can awaken the negative aspects of trauma and it's vital to identify and know your own and try to avoid them as best you can.

Everything I have explained so far pales into insignificance compared to the overwhelming feelings of guilt and remorse I felt from the minute I first realised what had happened after the accident, through the following years and it is still with me to a lesser extent now. I was a strong, assertive woman, well and truly able to make my own decisions. I was the one who decided to take up a dangerous sport, ignored all the signals not to jump that day, gave into peer pressure and put the parachute on my back. How could I then blame anyone else, especially not Joe, as if we had stuck to the rules of not jumping together and not when the boys were there, the final piece of the jigsaw when he came down in front of me would never have happened. At that time the children were my responsibility completely, I had let them down as a mother, been careless and reckless with their future and any positivity I got from jumping, including surviving when the odds were totally against me, felt totally insignificant. I thoroughly beat myself up.

On top of this I couldn't shake away the feeling of unworthiness of surviving such a dramatic accident when others wouldn't have, and I questioned myself continually as to why I deserved to be alive rather than them. I struggled over the years to find something "big" to justify being alive and couldn't ever find it. I was amazed at the physical feat's others achieved after sustaining major injuries where I had got away with relatively few, money raised for good causes through charities they set up and the obviously selfless goals they set for themselves, always aimed at helping others who had suffered in the same way as them.

It is strange that the perspectives of others can matter so much and how easy it was to add them on to my own guilty ones in the early days. I realised that there seemed to be a hierarchy of accidents; from those who were perceived to have brought it on themselves, to those who faced a tragic accident, that they had played no part in and therefore deserved more sympathy and understanding. *I have often wondered if I had been in a road traffic accident, or been in a situation where someone else was to blame, would I have felt differently?*

My lifestyle to date; with a teenage pregnancy, divorce and living with Joe behind me, had already put me in a box of disappointment and shame in the family, and I felt that the accident was another example of my irresponsible behaviour, sometimes verbalised by those who felt they had to give their opinion regardless of the hurt it would cause. It is well known that the baggage that is carried into the trauma will influence the extent to which the sufferer feels the negative effects and in my mind this played out in the amount of care and support I was given, the opinions and views on what I should do, or not, and the negative attitude relayed to women and mothers in dangerous sports in general, made for some difficult conversations. But then, this was my perception at that time when I felt so open and vulnerable to criticism, and I was supersensitive to everything that was said and done, I felt I had *"made my bed and had to lie in it"*. I had no fight then to challenge what others said, instead I listened and absorbed the words.

"How could you do this to yourself?", "Did you not think of your kids?" "I'll never forget hearing what had happened, I was upset, I knew you shouldn't have been doing skydiving.", "Be grateful you didn't die", "There's always someone worse off that yourself".

I know these were off-the-cuff remarks but when said to me time and time again it had the effect of laying the guilt on thickly; more than I needed, I had no headspace for anyone else's opinions, but they offered them anyway often making my head and body feel crammed with what I had done to everyone else by having the accident; their judgement, negative perceptions of me and accusations made me feel suffocated.

The first time I felt some relief was after a year, when the G.P. referred me to a counsellor. She was the only person at that time to not ask about my physical injuries or let me change the subject when I tried to deflect from the psychological pain by repeatedly asking, *"well, how do you feel about what has happened to you?"*. Finally, I could let my guard down and be honest, with someone who was independent and there to hear my innermost thoughts. I cried in session after session, for weeks, totally drained when she left, letting the tears flow, the best therapy I could have had.

No-one could have felt the overwhelming, sickening, and on-going feelings of guilt and shame more than Joe. We both blamed ourselves for different reasons, but his thoughts have never left and still haunt him today.

Joe's Trauma

"Joanne never accused me of causing the accident as she steadfastly believes it was only the final part of a much bigger picture and always took accountability for her choices. Nothing she ever said made me feel blamed, or that she resented me for what I had done. But I know it was that split-second decision I made in the air to come down in front of her, regardless of everything else that went before, I caused the accident, and I can't ever change that. I was constantly thinking of things I could have done to save her, maybe get to her more quickly to pull her chute or catch her in some way knowing that these are irrational thoughts but thinking them anyway. In that choice, that I made, I could have killed her, I changed her whole world, took away her love for skydiving

Even worse, I didn't admit my actions to anyone afterwards, until the immediate fallout of the accident was over and by that time everyone had naturally thought Joanne had made the mistakes, so when I did explain what happened no one really cared. I caused rows and hurt Joanne by always deflecting the blame onto her to make me feel better, "if you hadn't done that second turn the accident wouldn't have happened", but my confidence and belief in myself as a person and an instructor was shattered. I watched Joanne's frustration and annoyance that the whole truth wasn't out in the open but did nothing about it to begin with.

After several months I wrote a letter to the British Parachute Association to tell them what had happened to warn other instructors to take their actions more seriously. It was a huge relief to admit this and write it down, but the letter I received back, threatening to take away my instructor's rating and accusing me of doing this for financial gain, shocked me. I realised how casually the rules were taken in the skydiving world, no responsibility was taken and how quickly the barriers went up. After the accident Joanne's kit was taken away, under the guise that an investigation would be done, but we never heard of any outcome or saw any report, I have no idea if anything happened, or where the kit went. I carried on taking courses to make some money in the year afterwards, but my heart wasn't in it, and I gave up my instructors rating after a few more years.

On the weekend after the accident, I went back to the club and jumped, pretending nothing had changed and I'd be able to take up where I had left off. I had no idea I would be so traumatised; it was horrific. The person giving directions to the pilot stopped us immediately above the spot where Joanne had landing and looking out the door of the plane, I instantly remembered it all, feeling sick to my stomach and for the first time ever I didn't want to get out of the plane. Over all these years I have kept my silence, but I have never got the accident out of my head. The memories are vivid, of every aspect of the jump, from when I left on the plane, what happened next to when I found her on the ground came to the surface immediately in a terrifying flashback. I forced myself to get out of the plane, feeling a total emptiness that replaced any feelings of excitement, the whole jump became just a blur. The casual enjoyment had gone, the cockiness of being an instructor and experienced skydiver no longer there and it was no longer the rush it had been before. Over the next couple of years, I was no longer relaxed, overly conscious of any actions I took and the instructions I gave to others. I didn't do anything with others unless they were fully briefed so there would be no surprises and I knew they understood what they were to do. The number of jumps I did decreased dramatically and in 2011 I stopped after 964 jumps.

I was always going to look after Joanne and the kids, we already had a strong foundation of love and commitment, I never doubted this or considered leaving. Outwardly my life seemed to have changed little, but inwardly, I was in turmoil. I quickly put any feelings and memories of what I experienced that day away and wanted everyone to focus solely on Joanne, not me. I had let her down in our instructor/student relationship, but in the partnership of me and her I was never going to let that happen. By giving her the best, and making her my princess, I could repent, ease my remorse, and wrap her up in bubble-wrap to keep her safe. Of course, watching her struggle, in pain, frustrated, scared and insecure was so difficult to watch, knowing my part in it, but the old Joanne from before the accident was still there, the wicked sense of humour, glass always half-full, calmness and love with the kids, strength and unbelievable determination to recover which just made me love her more.

I wanted it to be just us, not wanting anyone else to get too close or give their opinions on what we were doing. At the same time, I felt in desperate need for our friends and struggled to keep the old life of parties and skydiving as good as it had been, holding on to our former life when it would never be the same again. Neither of us wanted to push them away and outwardly I don't think our friends would have thought either of us had changed, but internally we both had and so much. We kept friends in a group in the early days, never wanting to have the opportunity of one to ones in case they asked us how we felt, and we were very careful not to say anything when they were with us that would hurt each other, give them too much of the gory truth, or cause rows in front of them. We are lucky we still have the same brilliant friends who have stuck with us regardless."

- *Joe*

Time has moved on and the whole arena of research and treatment has expanded widely in twenty-five years, now it's easy to find out as much as any person wants to on any aspect of trauma, what they, or a loved one, can expect after the event, services and charities who can help and the understanding of the types and causes of trauma. I understand the therapies and treatments that could also work for me, but I don't want to go through more pain or disrupt and trigger events that I control, in the life I love. I can live with all the repercussions of the accident, knowing how complex they are and how they are now an ingrained part of my personality. Although it has taken years to reach this point, I have firmly placed the positives at the top of the pile and accept the negatives for the learning and insight they have brought. This is me, and actually, I quite like that.

Chapter Eight

Neither Here nor There

Over the past 25 years I have clung on to the belief that I am one of those special people who knows, with absolute certainty, that death is only a transition.

For years I have split the accident into two parts when discussing it with others; firstly, the list of physical injuries that they always wanted to know about were easy to describe and understand, and then the near-death experience story which I shared always and only in positive terms, never negative. Everything else around the short- and long-term trauma I avoided or ignored.

I understand why an experience like this would be interesting to others, understandably incomprehensible but fascinating at the same time. The picture of the place I painted can be imagined by others, but I found that it was the feelings and sensations that were hard to describe. I was in some other realm or dimension, transcending the boundaries of myself and the ordinary confines of time and space. I wasn't sure if this could be real either, even though I knew it was and as I researched for this book the similarities between my experience and that of others were undeniable.

Near-death experience events have been reported for hundreds of years, in all cultures, age is irrelevant, and they are no more likely to happen to the religious than the atheist. Over the past 100 years they have moved from the mythical to be named an NDE or "near-death experience" and common characteristics have been collated, some all of us will have heard of, or are familiar with. I experienced the majority of these; the overwhelming feelings of peace, timeliness, weightlessness, the sensation of being out of my body at the beginning of the experience, the vivid assault of colour and smells and the strong belief that if I took the path to the horizon, rather than the one that offered me a way back to my life, I would die on Earth, but be very much alive in wherever this place was. Unfortunately, not all NDE's are positive experiences, as mine was, and although not often spoken about, they can be so horrific that those going through them can feel that they are seeing hell and are struggling to get back. Understanding how vivid and long-lasting their memories will be I can't imagine how awful it would be to live with them every day.

Looking back on my life since the accident, I think I learned more from the NDE than any other part of my accident and its aftermath. It was so positive that it counteracted some of the most negative aspects of trauma. I do know I locked away the horrific memories and have recently been reminded that they are still there, in the deep recesses of my mind. They are fading memories whereas the certainty of the place I was in, with its vivid colours, beautiful smells, ultimate peace and an insight and knowledge that can't be explained away by any earthly theories I can recall with a clarity, as if it happened only yesterday. It remains my secret place to return to when inevitable life traumas and negativity touch my life.

Nearly everyone will have "a close brush with death" at some time in their life and it is common to hear, *"if I'd left the house 2 minutes earlier, I'd have been killed"*, or you step onto a road and the car you hadn't seen whizzes past, missing you by millimetres. These remind you of the precariousness and fragility of life but fade quickly. My experience is clear to me and has stayed with me for the rest of my life. I have related already the feelings, pain, and details of the accident as much as I can, but I am sure there are more that I have not memorised or that are insignificant. The memories of the near-death experience stand out and remain strong, easy to recall and with a description that never changes. Those images sit on the line between consciousness and unconsciousness in my brain, in the in-between place that is neither awake nor asleep.

I felt that I was still in that place immediately after I hit the ground, in those few seconds before the pain kicked in, as I lay on my back looking up at the sky. The shock of the physical accident was traumatic enough but to go from the best jump I had ever done, perfect turns in freefall, to panic, horror and certainty of death, to the most beautiful experience I had ever had then or since, and then to ground rush and slamming into the ground, all within seconds, was too overwhelming to take in.

When I was on my own the first couple of days in hospital, especially during the night when everything was quiet, except for the ward sounds and mummers coming from the nurses' station, I easily drifted in and out of the place where I had been. It was real, more than a morphine haze or dream, as I was still awake, fighting the traumatic memories that came with sleep and my mind full of unanswerable questions. Despite my uncertainty, I knew it was a real event, the same as all the others leading up to, and during the accident, but I wanted to know what it was and what it meant. I remember holding on to Joe's hand when I first saw him again, desperate for him to hear all the details, in case I forgot them later, and he has been the one person who has never doubted what I was saying.

I very quickly realised that from others I was going to be met with a myriad of responses, from belief to disbelief, interest to fear, or simply silence, as what can you say when someone tells you this? But usually, the subject was changed as quickly as possible, even before I finished recounting it. I could hear myself ask everyone who came near me about it, and then see their faces, as if I had lost my mind. The experience was so real and so powerful that I just wanted answers, but no one could give them to me. It didn't take long to stop questioning "why" to others, but the questions still swirled around in my head. I felt no one believed me and I didn't want anyone to belittle the experience, it deserved respect, and after a while it really didn't matter to me if people believed it had happened or not. The need for me to understand what I had experienced stayed with me through many questions; *"what if I had made a choice to stay, would that have been me wanting to die? If I had walked down the other path, would I not have come back? Did I see a glimpse of the afterlife, or was it a picture I conjured up in my mind of my own perfect heaven?"*

The usual visit of the hospital chaplain that everyone is offered happened a few days after the accident. I certainly didn't mind, I thought, "a new face to see, a bit of comfort perhaps". I tried to explain what I had experienced, but he was obviously very uncomfortable getting into the conversation at all. I wanted to know if this was a pathway to heaven and if the definite feeling of some greater entity than myself, something outside me, giving me the ultimate choice to live or die was God. The chaplain did listen, but then changed the subject, deflecting to my physical injuries and leaving after praying that I would heal quickly. I thought to myself that if he doesn't know, no one will. I was disappointed and confused, realising that I was probably going to have to work this one out on my own.

Over the years, as research and information improved, I never felt the need to study the multitude of explanations there are for this phenomenon or the never-ending information, podcasts, and books on the subject, but for this book I had to. As I delved through the evidence of disturbances of brain activity, lack of oxygen, too much carbon dioxide, hallucinations, reactions to extreme trauma, and many more, I knew they couldn't explain everything away, especially the mystical, spiritual elements and I was comfortable with my own unique experience and wanted to protect it as the positive, comforting side of the accident I believed it to be.

What struck me was how common near-death experiences are, but how little they are discussed generally and that they are non-existent in medical training, despite the many patients who will experience one whilst in medical care. Imagine if another phenomenon, or set of common features, was experienced by up to twenty per cent of the population worldwide. I'm sure the responses and attitudes would be very different as to what caused them, there may be less scepticism and greater understanding, and maybe those who have had one would be able to open up and share their stories, not hide them away. To live in a world where they don't have to face disbelief and isolation just because a near-death experience cannot be totally explained by science or biology.

Maybe it is that these experiences are too closely wrapped up in the reality and inevitability of death, that regardless of what a person believes happens after death, a vivid description from someone so sure they have seen that there is definitely more to life, can either confirm their views of an afterlife or make them revaluate their belief system, others explain it away as unbelievable or as having a rational biological explanation.

I was only 27 years when the accident happened, starting a new life after jumping some high hurdles along the way, believing I was invincible and certainly not going to die young, never thinking about it at all. I still had dreams of achieving great things, raising kids that would be great human beings, finding love and having an exciting life to reminisce over when I was old and grey. The thought of being in a situation where I would face death head-on, seconds in front of me, was a million miles away and I was totally unprepared. I was deluding myself, before the accident, that regardless of how much I had seen death, when my time came, I would go through this somehow differently from everyone else, with the minimum amount of pain, in a comfy bed with plumped up cushions, my nearest and dearest around me, or unexpectantly and immediately, without knowing it was coming. In any case, I planned it only to happen when I was older.

After the accident, this inevitable stage of life became more real to me, and I had a deeper understanding of the whole process, seeing it only as a bridge into another place, hopefully to the beautiful field I was in, taking the path into the horizon rather than the one to take me back, and hopefully when I'm ready next time.

As a nurse, seeing patients pass away in many different scenarios was an everyday event, but this was happening to them and not me, in hospital it was usually expected, planned for and when it happened it was easy for me to emotionally detach, move on to the next patient and, sadly, forget the details of the person who died. Stoicism was such an important part of the job as no one involved could possibly absorb all the individual stories of death or trauma they would see without seriously damaging their mental health and ability to look after those who were still alive. Often, I felt like bursting into tears or kicking and screaming on the floor when the news that would devastate a life was given, but I didn't crack or react and apart from how ridiculous it would look to see a nurse flailing about on the floor, it certainly wasn't what the patient would need at the time. Everything about death was medicalised around me, saving life was uppermost in my life, with all the equipment needed to save a person, oxygen, and fluids to ensure comfort when nothing more could be done. My job was to be the responder, the hand-holder and comforter, the shoulder to cry on, but only after everything had been tried to save the patient, even when it would have been much kinder not to. *However, I always wondered in some cases who we were saving the life for, does the person always have hope that medicine will save them, or such a strong will to live that they want to stay alive, no matter what they must do to try, no matter how harsh the treatment or resuscitation they will need? Is it for the relatives and loved ones who expect so much and understandably want to hold on to the person? Or is it for those clinicians treating the person who see death as the ultimate failure of their abilities and knowledge?*

After I returned to work my thought processes in relation to death had changed completely, as did my feelings of empathy and awareness of what a patient could be experiencing when they were passing away. I was sure that there was something more, as I had seen, when the person took their last breath. I had confirmation of this many times, when standing at the bedside, watching the calmness of realisation and resignation passing over a patient's face and feeling their energy leave the room, with only a body, a shell of a person, remaining. *Was this their soul, discarding a body they didn't need anymore? Were they going to heaven, or their energy simply dissipating into the air around them?*

By then I had never seen the natural dying process, without intervention of some type, and certainly had never heard a patient describe an out of body experience or NDE when they were resuscitated. This is so strange to me, as it has been reported that over 40% of clinical patients will have had one. Before experiencing my own, if a patient had told me about theirs, I probably would have dismissed it as unbelievable and carried on with the tasks and duties of a general nurse, focusing on their physical health, without much thought to what the patient was saying.

It was as my mother passed away a few years ago that I saw the natural death process in front of my eyes, for the first time, as she withdrew from the earthly activities she had enjoyed, disengaging from us more and more. The family were able to give her the comfort of being at home and looked after by us. We took turns to sleep in her room and one night her and I were having one of those in-depth life-chats you can only have in the dark, when she asked, *"how long will I be in this place for?"* Thinking she was asking how long she had left on earth I asked, *"what do you mean?"* knowing her time would be very short, but not wanting to tell her. *"I'm neither here nor there, not with you, but not there yet,"* she replied and when I asked her if she was scared, she simply said, *"no, it's fine"*.

In that moment I completely understood what she was describing, and I hoped above all that she was in her version of the beautiful place. My mother's passing was the first time I experienced grief for someone so close to me, and as heart-breaking as it was it's tinged with the positive belief that death is not the end or getting to a final destination but is only a transition.

I now have no fear of death and as much as I wanted to make sure that no one would let me die after the accident, underneath the initial shock and fear I knew I wasn't going to. I was given the fantastic opportunity to live, and I took it willingly.

I was given so much insight into a much larger universe than we can understand and, of course, that will have changed my belief in human existence. I'm a very ordinary person who was given a glimpse of the grand scheme of things and an understanding that each choice has repercussions, that we have been given free will and the responsibility to choose one of many paths we can go down every day. Everything is constant change and we create our own worlds within a bigger plan, where nothing is accidental or a result of chaos, and when I hear, *"it just wasn't your time"*, it may be true.

At that moment, when everything I knew on earth was stripped away, I felt complete trust in myself, whereas before I doubted many of the decisions I made and it was the only time I had a choice without restrictions, or other influences. In my life I was burdened by societies rules, rules from my childhood, an identity based on how well I did in my career, the house I had, the money I earned and a belief that I knew "right" from "wrong", but these became blurred and unimportant when replaced by the knowledge that, while we continually strive for something better, even waiting to die to get to a "better place", we are often never satisfied with what we have now and often do not notice the opportunities for love, learning, personal insight and contentment in the present. I saw this dissatisfaction many times as I rose up the ranks of the NHS, in some colleagues who would jump onto your shoulders to bypass you or bring you down, to reach where they wanted to go, using every negative personality trait to get there. I also worked with amazing people, with similar values to me or that I wanted to emulate; kindness, hard work and compassion and these values became the most important aspect of my life. I was given a special present and am a much better person for it.

Of course, I have had very bad times, been affected by disloyalty and others' behaviour, difficult events in life that take you off-guard, like everyone else. These I have had to deal with and accept as part of our existence, and they have affected my mental health afterwards, to the point of despair. My saving factor is that now I can pull myself out of these situations and create a new balance, remembering what was important to me then, I return to the knowledge that I've survived worse, continually have the will to live and know there is more to existence.

Relationships can be difficult. The superficial annoys me if that is all I get from others, it needs to be balanced with depth too, and as I result, I am much more comfortable with one to ones. The feelings of being disconnected from a group and "looking in", have never gone away, I always feel like a spare part in these situations. This could be a result of trauma or the near-death experience, but it reminds me of the horrible feeling of separation I felt when leaving the earth behind. This is difficult for me as I love being with and getting to know people and have no problems initiating a conversation so no one would know that it is still an effort I must make, or that I could easily isolate myself more and more.

There were also other mindset changes I noticed as I was recovering. The mundane, day-to-day activities and routine didn't matter as much as it had done before, in fact when I saw others taking these so seriously, I would be thinking, *"lighten up"*, *"don't sweat the small stuff"* and I am a lot calmer, sometimes appearing distracted or as if I am *"living in my head"*, or even not caring when I don't remember conversations or forget basic, practical things. I can't help thinking that life is far too short for those things and most of the time that's right. Luckily, I have Joe to take over and to put the diesel into my car, air into the tyres and all the other stuff I put into the *"I'll never get that time back,"* box. This works very well, until he goes away, and there have been times when I've run out of oil without realising it or the postman has rung the doorbell to tell me that he can't get any more post into the post-box, when I had thought we just didn't have any post!

I can problem-solve quickly both at home and at work and that became a real asset, giving me confidence and a feeling that there was nothing that I couldn't handle. A problem would come up to solve and immediately I would already know how to deal with it or come up with numerous solutions and then wait until others caught up with my thinking. Although Joe and I had real difficulties with money and uncertainties and worry for the future, I always found a way out, we were always OK.

"Did you see heaven?", "Did God give you the choice to live or die?" I have been asked these over the years, but this part of the experience confused my belief system rather than clarifying it. Those asking seemed to want to reaffirm their faith in the afterlife, but also that theirs was the only "true" religion. I had grown up in Protestant Christianity but rejected it in my late teens as I always felt I was fighting negativity, avoiding being "bad" with the guilt that brought, at all costs, and the distrust of other religions made me wonder if we were all serving the same God.

I can never know if this was heaven and God, but I know there is too big a picture to narrow it into one religion and I have found myself always looking for something more encompassing without having to pledge myself to a particular church with its own set of beliefs. If it was heaven, then heaven would have to be different for everyone as anyone who has experienced a near-death experience has an individual picture to paint, not one of a single heaven where everyone who gets there will see the same sights, as portrayed in many religious teachings. *Maybe I was in the antechamber and the horizon would lead to heaven, as I had understood it my whole life, up until then?*

So, I can't answer those questions and I am still exploring the strange phenomenon I went through and what it meant, but I have opened my mind to many more possibilities, I have a great sense of gratitude for life and will be forever in awe of the beautiful place I was in, the comfort it has given me over the years and the glimpse into a greater universe full of possibilities.

Chapter Nine

Bound Together

Others often ask us how we stayed together in those first few years, when the aftermath of the accident could well have pulled us apart, and on many occasions, we thought it would. We both suffered and handled the events in different ways, both equally terrified that our relationship wouldn't ride through the bad times, and even though I was the one who ended up with the injuries, physical and visible, Joe's experience was painful too. He had it all, the harsh memories, the terror during and after, the overwhelming guilt and shame for his part and fear that I wouldn't survive.

So much damage could have been done to our relationship in the first year after the accident, when I was totally dependent and neither of us had any awareness of how deeply trauma can manifest psychologically. We didn't know that the way we were feeling wasn't aimed at each other, but from emotional changes common after trauma, I wanted all my safety, protection, company, and love to come solely from Joe and reading from my diary I was insecure, paranoid that if we weren't skydiving together that we would have little else, and he would leave me. *Could I trust him when he was away from me? Would he meet someone else at the club, more attractive and alive with skydiving as I had once been? Was he only staying with me out of guilt?*

I sat at home thinking these destructive thoughts, driving myself crazy. I was angry, frustrated and scared without him, even if someone else was there to help me. *How could he still love a sport that nearly killed me?* When he got home, I picked his brain for details, looking for clues, always suspicious to the extent that he felt suffocated. I had no idea he was needing to hold onto something familiar and naturally needed his own time away to deal with his own thoughts. No matter how much he tried to reassure me and show so much affection, I was always fearful.

We had always been good at sharing our thoughts, feelings and hopes with each other, openly talking about our emotions all the time, but that changed dramatically. It seemed that there was more than an elephant in the room, it was a herd, and any row we had, no matter what it was about, reverted to the accident and always ended the same, *"if you hadn't come down in front of me"* and *"if you hadn't done that second turn"*. We had to stop doing this, and both of us wanted to get to the stage that we could share our painful feelings without recrimination, damaging blame and the hurt we were causing each other.

As the initial shock diminished, the negative effects of trauma began to fade and as I physically became more independent, we began to take stock of what had happened to us. Joe knew that the amount of care he had to give was short-term and I would push myself until I recovered. We were able to talk to each other enough to air the greatest obstacles, do something to resolve whatever was causing them, focus on the life we had now and start planning the future. It wasn't that we avoided talking about the accident in great depth, it was that we wanted to protect each other and after a while we never wanted to go back to those times again. There were a couple of pivotal times I remember, make or break decisions we had to take. I needed Joe to acknowledge what he had done in mid-air, which he did, and I had to learn how to control the negative emotions so that when they took over, I could change my thoughts to the positive and focus on the gratitude that I had survived. We learned on the way what triggered us both. I had to remember that I had had an extra dimension to my experience, my NDE, that he hadn't had, giving me a new perspective to life.

We both knew that our goal was to work together to provide a safe, nurturing family unit for the kids and, regardless of how long Joe would stay jumping, our life in skydiving had gone as we knew it, our focus and values had completely changed. Gone was the need to get our confidence, enjoyment, and self-belief from skydiving so we began to look for it from the other parts of our lives. Looking back now, skydiving was only a catalyst in our relationship and, as we moved on, I realised that it wasn't what kept us together after all.

Ultimately this is a love story, both of us were bound together completely by what happened in the sky that day and we already had a really strong foundation of love, passion, and a desire to stay together no matter what we faced. We never lost the intimacy, comfort and friendship that was vital to keep us together, that has only become more intense over the years.

We have achieved much together. Joe used the experiences of supporting me through physical and mental health issues to become a Mental Health nurse, and with his support I was able to deal with any ongoing effects of trauma enough to have a successful career in the NHS and start my own leadership business. I will be forever grateful we had each other through this journey and can't wait to see what we do next.

Act Four

The Flashback

"… Can you hear my voice?

This time this is my fight song

Take back my life song

Prove I'm alright song …"

- **Fight Song – Rachel Platten**

Chapter Ten

Triggering the Trauma

I thought I was doing fine, impressed with my ability to write memories and thoughts accumulated over the years, some jogged by researching and going through the diary I kept at the time, or reminiscing with friends about the life we had been caught up in. I was almost six months into my book writing journey and publication day was moving ever closer. They say the truth will set you free. My truth is a missing piece of the story and a flashback, that allowed me to see again the reality of what I had experienced, and finally describe the seconds when it all went wrong.

When I began to write I was hoping to work through any feelings or difficulties I might have hidden away, a cathartic exercise, one advocated by many as a tool that can help with recovery. I hadn't anticipated the type of journey it would be, rather like the heart-beat pattern on a monitor, over the line, under the line, high peaks, low peaks, and every peak in between. I hadn't expected the confidence I would have to summon up to believe in myself enough to put my story on paper and share my innermost thoughts. I thought I was strong, "healed", and that the book was nearly finished without denting myself too much. *How wrong could I be?*

In the back of my mind, I knew I was only showing the tip of the iceberg. When I started to write I felt like I was carefully stepping onto a large lake covered in ice, skimming over the surface, not knowing how thick the ice was, when it was going to crack and when I would fall through. Hoping I would get to the other side intact.

Well, for the first time in over two decades I fell in, right through the ice, deep into the water, unable to get out on my own. That's what trauma does, it creeps up on you and builds up inside, waiting for a trigger to switch it on and out it comes, like a demon from hell.

I had heard others advising me to, *"look after yourself"* and *"be careful not to re-traumatise yourself"*, but of course I knew better.

Triggers? What triggers? Don't they know I've managed this for all these years there's nothing else to come out? I've rung my memories dry.

I don't admit it often, but I was wrong, very wrong.

I was working long hours, one Friday afternoon I thought that I would stop writing for a while and do a little research of my own. Typing the search, *"how many people die skydiving?"* into google I expected numbers, that was all I was interested in, but instead of this I was scrolling down pages and pages of short news bulletin videos of the latest person to die. It was all too real. I think it could have been morbid curiosity, or maybe to test how much I'd moved on, but I clicked on the most recent one.

A beautiful female presenter was giving the report of an accident at DeLand Municipal Airport in Florida. Two skydivers' parachutes had become entangled, with one able to reflate his chute and survive whilst the other couldn't. I was transfixed by her mouth as she was talking, it looked like she was battling not to smile at the camera, remembering she was reporting something serious. She actually said, *"he hit the ground hard"* and died. What a stupid thing to say, of course he hit the ground hard, it was not going to be a tiptoe landing after all. The whole report was over in two minutes, it all seemed insignificant, just another tragedy and then move on.

And then it hit me. I felt such deep sadness, empathy and understanding like I never had before. So, so sad for the man who survived as he would be living with the trauma, and probably with survivor guilt for the rest of his life, and for the person who died unexpectedly, taking part in a sport he loved.

As I shut down the computer, unable to look at the screen anymore, I remembered others saying when things like this happened, *"at least he died doing something he loved, and it was quick".* Are they serious? Did they really think that when facing death they were thinking, *"this is wonderful, I'm really happy to be dying like this,"?* No, of course they weren't, and I could relate to them so deeply, as I got caught up in the story, but it was no longer about the men, their possible thoughts were melting into my own and I was transporting back to the horror of it all.

I began to write down feelings and thoughts that were coming to me, the words pouring out onto the page in seconds, as fast as I had fallen. Not the calming and beautiful feelings I describe when explaining my NDE, the part I prefer to talk about and cling onto as the good part of the otherwise horrific accident, but the full-blown, inescapable raw terror I felt. The part I didn't know was still there, inside, in the deepest recesses of my mind.

When I could I read what I had written, this is what I found:

"I'm feeling terrified, scared shitless, sick to the stomach, desperate to live, my life whirling around me in multicolour...faces, sounds, laughs, cries, thoughts, memories...bad, good, happy, sad, reaching out to catch them before they leave or my mind goes empty, not lose them all, but I can't grab them, steal them back...put everything back, there's no escape, it's out of my hands, no power, no control...please don't let there be nothing, let me stop just for a second, a moment...I'll never be bad again, I promise, I'm sorry...let me jump back, rewind this like a film and let me watch it again, slowly, able to pause when I want and fast-track the bad bits, reborn, grateful if you let me out of

here, never again, stop this happening, please, because I can't.

Take me away, I don't want to be here…I'm alone, no one to save me, lift me up and out, let this be someone else, someone I don't know, no, no one at all, never let anything bad happen again…I don't want to die, please don't let me now, I'm too young, this can't happen. I'm holding onto you boys, your faces, your smell, your joy, and boundless happiness, overflowing with life, future, hope and love. I'm going back, I'm coming back. They haven't gone out of my mind, flashing by, they're filling it up, overflowing, filling my senses…my mind, there when there is nothing else, I love you, I love you, I'm coming back, I'm not dying, not today, not now."

Epilogue

Closing the Circle

I did return to the site of the accident once again, when the story was told, with more understanding, insight, and acceptance than I had ever hoped for. It was a rough ride with highs and lows, new discoveries, uncovered memories and feelings that I thought were hidden for good, but there was one thing that I needed to do. I needed to leave something behind this time to close the circle and turn my back for the last time. Of course, I couldn't reach backwards to hug myself like I had wanted to when I first went back, I took a letter to the spot where I had landed, left it there and walked away.

Dear Joanne,

I can see you lying there on the ground, broken, shocked and scared, and I wish I could hold you and tell you it's going to be OK. Hold on to the feelings you have now, of relief and the realisation that you have survived, you have chosen to live, that your love for your children and will to go on have saved you. You are going to make an unbelievable recovery and make a difference to so many people who will know you.

You will see Natalie and your boys grow up, have another daughter, all of whom will grow up to be adults to be proud of and lovely human beings. The generations will stretch out with grandchildren who you will adore and who will be a big part of your life. You will hold on to the relationship you have with Joe, even though you will doubt it can survive at times, and which will be full of laughs, love, passion and support for each other, true soulmates, and best friends. You are bound together by what has happened to you both in these last few minutes and for years to come.

The fall-out of this accident will hopefully be the worst thing you go through in your lifetime, life is inevitably tough and difficult, as you already know, but you have the resilience, ability to adapt and change, perseverance, a passion to succeed and inner strength to move on from this. You will learn so much from this experience, learn what is important to you to help you in your life and career and it will change your thinking, in so many ways.

But you're definitely not perfect, even if you'd love to be, (or think you are!) and there are some golden rules that could have made your recovery so much easier:

- ❖ *Don't feel you haven't done enough to justify your survival by doing something you consider exceptional or must prove yourself a better person than before. You will make a difference to those you love and those around you. You don't have to do something great to be great.*
- ❖ *Tell your story when you want to, how you want to and to those who will treat it with the respect it deserves.*

❖ *Try not to focus on the negatives, difficulties, or hardships you have been through too often, as these will become dominant and stay with you for years, whereas the good and funny times, positive new memories and just being alive will take second place and be easily forgotten.*

❖ *Although you'll not know it for several years, the physical, emotional, and psychological changes you don't understand now are a mixture of everything you have gone through and will fade with time. Keep learning, as understanding what's going on will be eye-opening.*

❖ *Give yourself a break. Have a good hard look at your reality, what you can control, influence, or change and what you can't. Say to yourself, "is this going to help or harm me?" to decide which path to take. Remember what hurts us can also help us, so use every experience, good or bad to learn and grow from.*

❖ *You have no control over what others say or do, but you can let them know how it affects you, find your voice. Be brave, instead of harbouring resentment, guilt and shame heaped on by yourself and others. It's not all about you! Be fair and compassionate to those around you as they have experienced your accident in their own way too.*

❖ *Don't be afraid of your "Near-death Experience" or expect others to see what you saw or be able to explain it. Take it for the beautiful, comforting event that it was and go there when you need to.*

And finally, be proud of what you have achieved and the successes that you have had. You survived hitting the ground at over 100mph, where others may not have and that is amazing. That may have been fate, good luck or God saving you, but you don't need to question why, just enjoy that you did.

Joanne and Joe

Connect with Joanne

Joanne is an author and speaker who incorporates her personal experience as told in this book, and the learning she gained, to provide motivational talks, workshops and learning events, with her unique take on many topics, including;

- Living with, and learning from, Trauma

- Overcoming adversity, building resilience

- Near-Death Experiences

- When the Carer becomes the Cared-for

- Building Emotional Intelligence

- Inspirational Leadership

....and many more

Joanne has a wide audience base, from charities focusing on mental health and trauma, healthcare professions and their training organisations, private and public sector executives, and teams, to event organisers who are looking for a unique story from a key-note speaker. Joanne is also available for interviews with media and networks.

Find out more and connect with Joanne visit her website **JoanneMcConville.com** or get in touch by email: info@JoanneMcConville.com

Clarity Change

Joanne is passionate about great leadership and working with individuals and teams to make their work and homelife the best it can be. In 2019 she founded Clarity Change to bring her 30 years of experience in the NHS, from nursing on the front-line to senior management, to help private and public organisations focus on leadership, culture, and service improvement. She encourages and supports leaders to take a different, and more interesting, approach to leadership development and change management.

Joanne strongly believes that survival in life, and in the workplace, needs the same skills of focus, setting goals, positivity, adaptability, resilience, and personal growth to cope with all the ups and downs that we will inevitably experience in the future.

Please see her business website, **ClarityChange.co.uk** or email info@claritychange.co.uk to learn more about how she can help you.

Acknowledgements

This book would never have become more than a jumble of memories and an old diary if I hadn't had the encouragement and interest of many people down the years, willing me on to put my story down on paper. From the start of my book-writing journey, through to its completion, there are some key people that I would like to thank for helping me to write the first line, sharing ideas and experiences, supporting me through the difficult chapters and most of all, listening to me talking endlessly about the book and its progress.

Top of the list must be Joe and my family. Joe for his unwavering love, belief in me and for pushing me to carry on when I wanted to stop. Natalie, Aaron, Matthew, and Alex who shared their memories of that time in their lives and gave me unconditional support to write the book, and to Ella who was curious to find out what happened before she was born, held my hand when I went back to the scene of the accident, and kept me writing.

My grandchildren, Chloe, Joshua and Emma, (and any others who come along), who add so much to my life. I hope the messages in this book will help and comfort you, whatever you decide to do in the future.

My father, brother and sister who encouraged me to write the book in the first place and let me dominate all conversations for the past year, and my late mother who I know would have advised and encouraged me throughout.

Our closest friends, who have been with Joe and I from our jumping days to now, and who we couldn't have been without through my recovery and always. The new friends we have met along the way, who have been fascinated in my story and have encouraged me to put it down on paper.

Heather Shields, who has edited and published this book, for her unbelievable patience and knowledge in a completely new world for me and her friendship throughout. She has gained an insight into my thought processes that few understand to help me move me from "telling" the story to "showing" the story. I wouldn't have been able to do this without her.

Mabel Doole who provided me with research on trauma and near-death experiences and helped me to begin my journey of understanding around the impact these had on my life.

Daniela Balmaverde the artist who turned "my piece of sky" into the fantastic book cover.

Miriam Stevenson who helped me develop websites, taught me to use social media and put up with numerous changes and drafts. Her ability to turn my ideas into reality was brilliant.

Camilla Long for her knowledge on public speaking that has built my confidence and self-belief immeasurably to the point where I can follow my dream of using my story to help and inform others.

Turan Mirza whose hypnotherapy and support gave me the confidence to return to the site of the accident.

My independent readers whose feedback gave me so much confidence and encouragement to publish.

And finally, my readers. I hope you will be uplifted, inspired to carry on and use my experience to help you in your future.

From the Album

1992 Left: Alex, me, Aaron & Matthew

Right: Newspaper picture of Matthew and I before the charity jump

Left: Newspaper picture of Joe with his Instructor's certificate, 1993.

Right: Joe, me and the boys at my brother's wedding, 1997

Joe and Stevie jumping out of
a Cessna 206

Joe, Willie, Evan and Stevie's
four-way

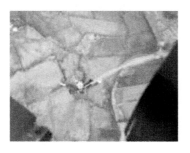

One of my first static-line jumps

Above: Joe after a jump into
Fall's Park, Belfast

Left: Our GAVID, the
Cessna

In 1994

Above: Me about to leave the plane

Below: Out on the step waiting to let go

Our Wedding Day, 1997

Top left: Natalie

Top right: Joe and I

Left: (from left) Alex, Matthew

and Aaron

Below: The Blueskies Gang

Above: (from left) My sister Karen, Mum, me, brother Robert and Dad, 2002

Ella Rose, 2020

Above left: Me with our granddaughter, Chloe, 2021

Above: Our Grandson, Joshua, 2021

Left: Our Granddaughter, Emma, 2022

Going back for the first time - The Return, 2020:

Left: The spot where I landed
Middle: The site of the accident
Bottom pic: The trees surrounding the place where I landed, top left, and the end of the runway

Printed in Great Britain
by Amazon

79442809R10164